The Essential Guide
TO THE
Anglican Communion

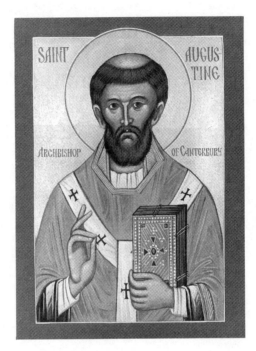

The Essential Guide
TO THE
Anglican Communion

compiled by James Rosenthal

THE ANGLICAN COMMUNION SECRETARIAT
LONDON

MOREHOUSE PUBLISHING

Morehouse Publishing
P.O. Box 1321
Harrisburg, PA 17105

Morehouse Publishing is a division of the Morehouse Group.

Printed in the United States of America

Cover design by Corey Kent

Photographs courtesy of the Anglican Communion Office.

"Compass Rose Flower" is reprinted from the Michaelmas 1997 edition of The Anglican Digest and used by permission of SPEAK.

"What Anglicans Believe" is reprinted from David L. Edwards, *What Anglicans Believe,* © 1996 and used by permission of Forward Movement Publications.

The Catechism from the Church of the Province of Southern Africa is reprinted from *An Anglican Prayer Book,* 1989, © Provincial Trustees of the Church of the Province of Southern Africa. Used by permission.

"Anglican Temperament" is reprinted from John H. Westerhoff, *A People Called Episcopalians,* St. Luke's Press, revised 1998. St. Luke's Episcopal Church, 435 Peachtree Street, NE, Atlanta, GA 30365-6401.

"Glossary of Terms" is modified from *A–Z of the Church of England,* © Church House Publishing, London. Used by permission.

The Lambeth Hymn, "Affirm Anew the Threefold Name," is used by permission of Hope Publishing Co., Carol Stream, IL 60188, for U.S. and Canada, and by permission of Timothy Dudley-Smith for all other world rights.

Library of Congress Cataloging-in-Publication Data

The essential guide to the Anglican communion / edited by James Rosenthal.
    p.   cm.
    Includes bibliographical references.
    ISBN 0-8192-1743-3 (pbk.)
    1. Anglican Communion.   I. Rosenthal, James.
BX5005.E87   1998
283—dc21   98-17577
                                                                              CIP

Contents

Introduction

Canon James M. Rosenthal

∽

THIS ESSENTIAL ANGLICAN HANDBOOK is an up-to-date guide to faith and practice in the worldwide Anglican Communion. Compiled as a document to complement the Lambeth Conference 1998, the book contains photos from around the globe, maps, essential addresses, and data, including basic statistics, a list of the Primates, and the soon-to-be thirty-eight Provinces of the Church. Also contained in this handbook are historical Anglican documents, a lecture text of the Archbishop of Canterbury, and the text of a provocative sermon by the Secretary General of the Anglican Communion.

The comprehensiveness of Anglicanism is reflected in an essay on Anglican worship by the Coordinator of Liturgical Studies, and several hymns are included; the text of the special hymn for the Lambeth Conference, by Bishop Timothy Dudley-Smith, makes its first appearance in print.

Explanations are given on the work of the four instruments of unity that help cement the ministry and global nature of the Communion. These four instruments are:

The Lambeth Conference

The Anglican Consultative Council

The Primates Meeting

The Archbishop of Canterbury (as *Primus Inter Pares*)

It is hoped that this volume provides information that is useful for clergy and laity throughout the Church.

Preface

Archbishop of Canterbury, George L. Carey

THROUGH MY MANY VISITS to different parts of the Anglican Communion I am very aware of the interdependence that underlies our unity and supports our mission and service in God's world today. We need each other. Our Anglican Tradition has much to offer in its proclamation of the gospel and in its understanding of reconciled diversity.

It is my hope that *The Essential Guide to the Anglican Communion* will enrich the life of our global family by telling some of the stories of those who serve the Anglican Communion in a variety of ministries. I would also hope that those enquiring about the Anglican expression of the Christian faith will find that this concise and easy-to-use book serves as a vehicle to encourage them on their journey. By taking the time to learn more about ourselves, perhaps we can all more readily and more ably pray for one another, and work for the good of the body and for the whole of God's creation.

"Come, Holy Spirit, kindle in us the fire of your love."

The Liturgical Year

∽

THE 1993 JOINT MEETING of the Primates of the Anglican Communion and the Anglican Consultative Council adopted principles, criteria, and a process for the recognition of godly men and women by including them in the calendars of the Churches for remembrance. The meeting affirmed that the revision of calendars is an ongoing process, one of the ways in which the Church holds the Christian hope for the people of God, to enable their growth as a Holy Temple in the Lord (Ephesians 2:12).

In part, the resolution says, the commemoration of holy people is always an act of anamnesis. We remember not only the person's historical events but also the power of grace in their lives and, consequently, of Christ in us, the hope of glory. A calendar is an instrument for worship, much the same as a eucharistic prayer. We may learn from both, but we use them primarily for worship. Calendars should be developed to honour and expend the thankful remembering of Christian people. While commemorations begin at the local level, among those who knew and remember a holy person, it is not inappropriate for them to be spread more widely, especially if the lifestyle of holiness expressed in the life of a person addresses in a striking way the aspirations of a particular generation of Christians.

The following traits will be found in those who are commemorated:

1. Heroic faith

2. The fruits of the Spirit

3. Christian engagement

4. Recognition by the Christian community

This calendar is a compilation of dates commemorated in various prayer books and service books of the Churches of the Anglican Communion. It is not to be considered complete or directive, but is to be used to aid worship and devotion in private and public prayer and to show the diversity of commemoration throughout the Communion.

JANUARY

1st	Holy Name
4th	Seraphim of Sarov
6th	Epiphany
10th	William Laud
12th	Aelred, Abbot of Rievaulx, 1167
13th	St. Kentigern (Mungo) Scotland
14th	Richard Benson of Cowley
18th	The Confession of Saint Peter
20th	Sebastian, Martyr
23rd	Yona Kanamuzeyi, Deacon and Martyr, Africa
25th	The Conversion of Saint Paul
30th	Charles Stuart, Martyr

FEBRUARY

1st	St. Brigid, Ireland
2nd	Candlemas: The Presentation of Our Lord in the Temple
3rd	Saints and Martyrs of Europe
5th	Martyrs of Japan
13th	Absalom Jones, Priest, 1818
14th	Valentine, Martyr
15th	Thomas Bray, Missionary
17th	Janani Luwum, Archbishop of Uganda, Martyr
24th	Saint Matthias the Apostle
27th	George Herbert, Parish Priest, Poet (d. 1633), and all Saintly Parish Priests

MARCH

1st	St. David
7th	Perpetua and Her Companions

MARCH (continued)

9th   Maqhamusela Khanyile of Zululand, Martyr
13th Kereopa and Manihera of Taranaki, Martyrs at Turangi, 1847
17th St. Patrick
19th St. Joseph
21st Thomas Cranmer, Archbishop of Canterbury, Martyr and Liturgist (d. 1556)
25th The Annunciation of Our Lord to Our Lady
29th John Keble, Pastor
31st John Donne, Poet

APRIL

1st   Frederick Denison Maurice, Priest, 1874
3rd   Richard of Chichester, Bishop, 1253
8th   Saints and Martyrs of the America
9th   Dietrich Bonhoeffer, Pastor and Martyr
11th George Augustus Selwyn, Bishop and Missionary New Zealand
19th Alphege
21st Anselm, Archbishop of Canterbury
23rd St. George
24th Toyohiko Kagawa, Teacher, Evangelist, Japan, 1960
25th St. Mark the Evangelist

MAY

1st   SS Philip and James, Apostles
2nd   St. Athanasius
8th   Dame Julian of Norwich, c. 1417
18th Rota Waitoa, Te matumau o nga minita Maori, the first Maori ordained in New Zealand, 1853
24th Mother Edith, founder of the Community of the Sacred Name, Christchurch, 1922
24th Jackson Kemper, First Missionary Bishop in the United States, 1870
25th The Venerable Bede
26th St. Augustine of Canterbury
31st The Visitation of the Blessed Virgin Mary

JUNE

1st   Justin, Martyr
3rd   The Martyrs of Uganda, 1886
9th   St. Columba
11th   St. Barnabas the Apostle
15th   Evelyn Underhill, Mystical Writer
18th   Bernard Mizeki, Martyr, Mashonaland
19th   Sadhu Sundar Sigh, Teacher, Evangelist, India, 1929
22nd   St. Alban the Martyr, Britain
24th   The Birth of John the Baptist
29th   SS Peter and Paul, Apostles

JULY

11th   Benedict, Religious
20th   Elizabeth Cady Stanton, Amelia Bloomer, Sojourner Truth,
       and Harriet Ross Tubman
22nd   St. Mary Magdalene
25th   St. James the Apostle
26th   Parents of the Blessed Virgin Mary
29th   William Wilberforce, Philanthropist

AUGUST

1st   Holy Men and Women of the Old Testament
6th   The Transfiguration of Our Lord
9th   Mary Sumner, Mothers' Union
13th   Florence Nightingale, Social Reformer
14th   Martin Luther King, Worker for civil liberties (d. 1968)
14th   Jonathan Myrick Daniels
15th   St. Mary the Virgin—Principal Feast
18th   William Porcher DuBose, Priest, 1918
23rd   Rose of Lima
24th   St. Bartholomew the Apostle
27th   Thomas Gallaudet, 1902, and Henry Winter Syle, 1890

SEPTEMBER

1st   David Pendleton Oakerhater, Deacon and Missionary, 1931
2nd   The Martyrs of New Guinea
7th   The Saints and Martyrs of the Pacific
8th   The Birth of Mary

SEPTEMBER (continued)

9th   Mother Esthern CHN, founder of the Community of the Holy Name, Melbourne (d. 1931)

12th   John Henry Hobart, Bishop of New York, 1830

14th   The Exaltation of the Holy Cross

16th   St. Ninian

17th   Hildegarde of Bingen, Mystic Religious, 1179

18th   Churchill Julius, Bishop, first Archbishop of New Zealand, 1938

19th   Theodore of Tarsus, Archbishop of Canterbury

20th   John Coleridge Patteson, Bishop and Martyr, Melanesia

21st   St. Matthew the Apostle and Evangelist

26th   Lancelot Andrewes, Bishop of Winchester

27th   Martyrs of Melanesia

29th   Michaelmas: St. Michael and All Angels

OCTOBER

1st   Mother Marie-Joseph Aubert, Religious, Social Reformer, 1926

4th   Francis of Assisi, Friar

6th   William Tyndale. Translator

15th   Our Lady of Walsingham (or September 23)

15th   Teresa of Avila, Nun, 1582

16th   Hugh Latimer and Nicholas Ridley, Bishops, Martyrs

18th   St. Luke the Evangelist

19th   Henry Martyn, Missionary to the East

23rd   St. James of Jerusalem

24th   United Nations, inaugurated 1945

28th   SS Simon and Jude, Apostles

29th   James Hannington and His Companions, Martyrs

30th   Holy Men and Women of the New Testament

NOVEMBER

1st   All Saints' Day

2nd   All Souls' Day

3rd   Richard Hooker, Anglican Apologist, Teacher

7th   Willibrord, Bishop, Holland

8th   Saints and Martyrs (of our time, of the Anglican Communion)

11th   Martin of Tours

NOVEMBER (continued)

14th Samuel Seabury, Bishop in America
16th St. Margaret of Scotland
22nd Cecelia, Virgin and Martyr
22nd James Noble, first indigenous Australian ordained (d. 1941)
28th Kamehameha and Emma, King and Queen of Hawaii, 1864, 1885
30th St. Andrew the Apostle

DECEMBER

1st   Nicholas Ferrar, Deacon and Religious
3rd   Saints and Martyrs of Asia
5th   Peter Masiza, Priest
6th   Nicholas, Bishop of Myra
8th   The Conception of the Blessed Virgin Mary
12th Our Lady of the Americas
13th Lucy
21st St. Thomas the Apostle
25th The Nativity of Our Lord: Christmas
26th St. Stephen, Deacon and Martyr
27th St. John the Evangelist
28th The Holy Innocents
29th St. Thomas Becket
30th Josephine Butler, Social Reformer

THE SUNDAYS OF ADVENT

The Christmas Season
The Epiphany
The Baptism of Our Lord
The Epiphany Season (Ordinary Time)

THE SUNDAYS IN LENT

Holy Week
Easter: The Resurrection of Our Lord
Easter Week

THE SUNDAYS OF EASTER

Ascension Day
The Day of Pentecost: Whitsunday

THE SUNDAYS OF EASTER (continued)
Trinity Sunday
Corpus Christi
The Season after Trinity (or Pentecost, Ordinary Time)
The Season before Advent (of the Kingdom)
Christ the King

OTHER DAYS
National Days
Thanksgiving
Mothering Sunday (Mother's Day)
Bible Sunday
Dedication Festival
Rogation Days
Ember Days
Anglican Communion Sunday
Christian Unity Octave

Anglican Identity

∽

As a world family of churches, the Anglican Communion has more than 70 million adherents in 160 countries. In the Sudan.

ANGLICAN WORLD

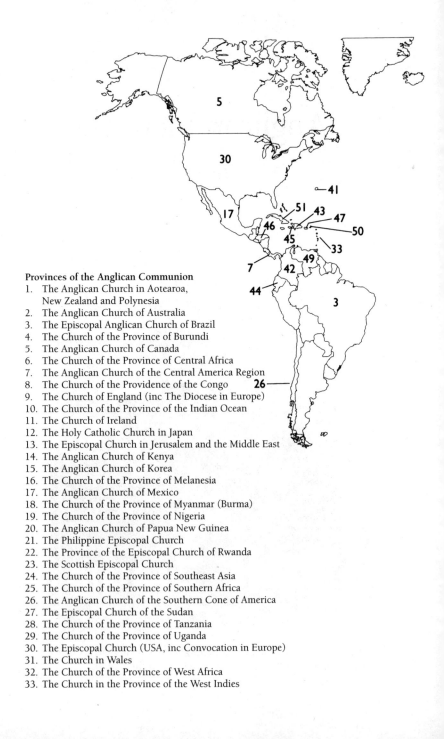

Provinces of the Anglican Communion
1. The Anglican Church in Aotearoa, New Zealand and Polynesia
2. The Anglican Church of Australia
3. The Episcopal Anglican Church of Brazil
4. The Church of the Province of Burundi
5. The Anglican Church of Canada
6. The Church of the Province of Central Africa
7. The Anglican Church of the Central America Region
8. The Church of the Providence of the Congo
9. The Church of England (inc The Diocese in Europe)
10. The Church of the Province of the Indian Ocean
11. The Church of Ireland
12. The Holy Catholic Church in Japan
13. The Episcopal Church in Jerusalem and the Middle East
14. The Anglican Church of Kenya
15. The Anglican Church of Korea
16. The Church of the Province of Melanesia
17. The Anglican Church of Mexico
18. The Church of the Province of Myanmar (Burma)
19. The Church of the Province of Nigeria
20. The Anglican Church of Papua New Guinea
21. The Philippine Episcopal Church
22. The Province of the Episcopal Church of Rwanda
23. The Scottish Episcopal Church
24. The Church of the Province of Southeast Asia
25. The Church of the Province of Southern Africa
26. The Anglican Church of the Southern Cone of America
27. The Episcopal Church of the Sudan
28. The Church of the Province of Tanzania
29. The Church of the Province of Uganda
30. The Episcopal Church (USA, inc Convocation in Europe)
31. The Church in Wales
32. The Church of the Province of West Africa
33. The Church in the Province of the West Indies

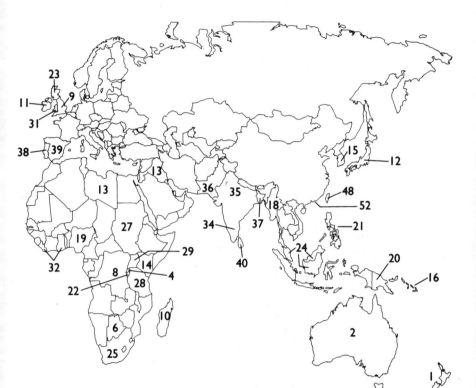

The Churches in which Anglicans joined other denominations
34. The Church of South India
35. The Church of North India
36. The Church of Pakistan
37. The Church of Bangladesh

Churches outside provinces but in the Anglican Communion under the Archbishiop of Canterbury
38. The Lusitanian Church of Portugal
39. The Spanish Reformed Episcopal Church
40. The Church of Ceylon (Sri Lanka)
41. Bermuda

ECUSA (outside the borders of USA)
42. Colombia
43. Dominican Republic
44. Ecuador
45. Haiti
46. Honduras
47. Puerto Rico
48. Taiwan
49. Venezuela
50. Virgin Islands

Autonomous, under Metropolitan Council of the primates of the West Indies, Canada and ECUSA Prov.IX
51. Cuba

Province information
52. Hong Kong (Province in Formation)
   Holy Catholic Church in China
   (now post denominational church)

9,30 The Convocation of American Churches in Europe includes parishes in Belgium, France, Germany, Italy and Switzerland that are under the jurisdiction of the Presiding Bishop of the Episcopal Church USA. The Church of England, Diocese in Europe has parishes in virtually all countries in Western, Central and Eastern Europe and in Turkey and Morocco.

Churches and Provinces
in Many Nations

The Anglican Church in Aotearoa, New Zealand, and Polynesia

Members: 220,659

Formerly known as the Church of the Province of New Zealand, the Church covers 106,000 square miles and includes the countries of New Zealand, Fiji, Toga, Samoa, and the Cook Islands. It was established as an autonomous Church in 1857. A revised constitution adopted in 1992 reflects a commitment to bicultural development that allows freedom and responsibility to implement worship and mission in accordance with the culture and social conditions of the Maori, white European, and Polynesian membership.

Primate and Archbishop of New Zealand
The Most Rev. Brian Newton Davis (Bishop of Wellington)
PO Box 885, Hastings, New Zealand
Tel: (64) 06 878 7902
Fax: (64) 06 878 7905

The Anglican Church of Australia

Members: 3,998,444

The Church came to Australia in 1788 with the "First Fleet," which was made up primarily of convicts and military personnel. Free settlers soon followed. A General Synod held in 1872 formed the Australian Board of Missions; missionary work among the aborigines and Torres Strait Islanders was key to the growth of the Church. The Church became fully autonomous in 1962 and in 1978 published its first prayer book. A second Anglican prayer book was published in 1996.

The Anglican Church of Australia is part of the Christian Conference of Asia and of the Council of the Church of East Asia. Links with the churches of New Guinea, Melanesia, and Polynesia are strong.

Primate of the Anglican Church of Australia
The Most Rev. Keith Rayner (Archbishop of Melbourne)
St. Paul's Cathedral Building, 209 Flinders Lane, Melbourne,
  Victoria 3000
Tel: (61) 03 9653 4220
Fax: (61) 03 9650 2184

The Church of Bangladesh

Members: 12,500

Bangladesh was part of the State of Pakistan, which was partitioned from India in 1947. After the civil war between East and West Pakistan ended in 1971, East Pakistan became Bangladesh. The Church of Bangladesh is one of the United Churches, formed by a union of Anglicans with Christians of other traditions.

Bishop of Dakha
Moderator, The Most Rev. Barnabas Dwijen Mondal
St. Thomas Church, 54 Johnson Rd., Dakha 1100, Bangladesh
Tel: (880) 2 234650
Fax: (880) 2 238218

Anglican Church of Bermuda

Members: 24,800

This extraprovincial diocese is under the metropolitical jurisdiction of the Archbishop of Canterbury.

Bishop of the Anglican Church of Bermuda
The Rt. Rev. A. Ewen Ratteray
Bishop's Lodge, PO Box HM 769, Hamilton HM CX, Bermuda
Tel: (441) 292 2967
Fax: (441) 296 0592

The Episcopal Anglican Church of Brazil
(Igreja Episcopal Anglicana Do Brasil)

Members: 103,021

Expatriate Anglican chaplaincies were established in Brazil in 1810, with missionary work beginning in 1889, after the separation of Church and State. The Province, which is one of the few Portuguese-speaking churches in the Communion, became autonomous in 1965. In 1990, Brazil's economic and social problems prompted the Partners in Mission Consultation to focus on three priorities: education, service, and expansion. *Estandarte Cristao,* the monthly Church journal based in Porto Alegre, has been published since 1893.

Primate of the Episcopal Anglican Church of Brazil
The Most Rev. Glauco Soares de Lima (Bishop of Sao Paulo)
Rua Comendador Elias Zarzur
1239, 04736-002 Sao Paolo, Brazil
Tel: (55) 011 246 0383/(55) 011 246 2180
Fax: (55) 011 246 2180

The Church of the Province of Burundi

Members: 425,000

There are approximately 170,000 Anglicans out of a population of just over 6 million in Burundi. The Catholic White Fathers came to Burundi at the time of early exploration but were met with a hostile reaction. In the closing years of the last century, the Roman Catholic Church was established and is still the largest Christian church, with 62% of the population baptised. A Protestant Alliance was formed in 1935 comprising Baptists, Free Methodists, and others, and there has been a healthy conversion rate, especially in the 1940s and 1950s, building on early medical and mission school work. However, momentum in this growth has ceased and African church and youth leaders and evangelists are now looking for further training to help them build on this work.

Primate of the Church of the Province of Burundi
The Most Rev. Samuel Sindamuka (Archbishop of Burundi)
(Bishop of Matana)

BP 1300, Avenue d'Angola, Bujumbra, Burundi
Tel: (257) 224 389
Fax: (257) 229 129

The Anglican Church of Canada

Members: 740,262

The Anglican Witness in Canada started in the eighteenth century with the Church Missionary Society and the United Society for the Propagation of the Gospel. The Eucharist was first celebrated in Frobisher Bay in 1578; the first Church building was St. Paul's, Halifax, in 1750. The Church includes a large number of the original inhabitants of Canada—Indians, Inuit, and Meti—and has been a strong advocate of their rights. A book of alternative services was published in 1985.

Primate of the Anglican Church of Canada
The Most Rev. Michael G. Peers
600 Jarvis Street, Toronto, ON M4Y 2J6
Tel: (416) 924 9192 x276
Fax: (416) 968 7983

The Church of the Province of Central Africa

Members: 600,000

The Province includes Botswana, Malawi, Zambia, and Zimbabwe. The first Anglican missionary to Malawi was Bishop Charles Mackenzie, who arrived with David Livingstone in 1861. The Province was inaugurated in 1955 and has a movable bishopric. The countries forming the Province are very different. Zambia and Botswana suffer the difficulties of rapid industrialization, along with underdeveloped, thinly populated areas. In Malawi, 30 percent of the adult males are away as migrant laborers in other countries at any given time. Zimbabwe is experiencing problems of social adjustment after independence.

Archbishop of the Province of Central Africa
The Most Rev. Walter P. K. Makhulu (Bishop of Botswana)
PO Box 769, Gaborone, Botswana
Tel: (267) 353 779
Fax: (267) 352 075

The Anglican Church of the Central American Region (Iglesia Anglicana de la Region Central de America)

Members: 13,409

The newest Province of the Anglican Communion is made up of the dioceses of Guatemala, El Salvador, Nicaragua, Costa Rica, and Panama. With the exception of Costa Rica, all had been part of the Episcopal Church of the United States of America. The Church was introduced by the Society for the Propagation of the Gospel when England administered two colonies in Central America, Belize (1783–1982) and Miskitia (1740–1894). In later years Afro-Antillean people brought their Anglican Christianity with them. The Province is multicultural and multiracial and is committed to evangelization, social outreach, and community development.

The Most Rev. Cornelius Wilson
Primate of IARCA (Bishop of Costa Rica)
Iglesia Episcopal Costarrica
Apartado 2773, 1000 San Jose, Costa Rica
Tel: (506) 225 0209
Fax: (506) 253 8331

Hong Kong and Macao

Members: 29,000

The history of the Church dates back to the mid-nineteenth century; missionaries were provided by the American Church, the Church of England, the Church of England in Canada, the Church of Ireland, the Churches of Australia and New Zealand. Western missionaries withdrew in 1950. All Churches were closed in 1966 and did not begin to reopen until 1979. Most denominations then joined the China Christian Council. The suppression of the pro-democracy movement in 1989 resulted in stricter regulations for religious groups. Today members of the Chung Hua Sheng Kung Hui (the Holy Catholic Church in China) are found in the post-denominational Church, the Three-Self Movement, except for in Hong Kong, which returned to Chinese sovereignty in 1997, and in Macao, which will be returned to China by Portugal in 1999.

Archbishop (Province in formation)
The Most Rt. Rev. Peter Kwong (Bishop of Hong Kong and Macao)

Council of the Church of East Asia
Bishop House, 1 Lower Albert Rd., Hong Kong
Tel: (852) 2526 5355
Fax: (852) 2521 2199

The Church of the Province of the Congo

Members: 300,000

Ugandan evangelist Apolo Kivebulaya established the Anglican presence in Zaire in 1896. The Church reached the Shaba region in 1955, but evangelization did not progress on a large scale until the 1970s. Following independence, the Church expanded and formed dioceses as part of the Province of Uganda, Burundi, Rwanda, and Boa-Zaire. The new Province was inaugurated in 1992 and changed its name in 1997.

Archbishop of the Province of the Congo
The Most Rev. Patrice Byankya Njojo (Bishop of Boga)
CAZ-Bunia, PO Box 21285, Nairobi, Kenya

The Episcopal Church of Cuba

Members: 3,000

The Episcopal Church of Cuba is under a Metropolitan Council in matters of Faith and Order. Council members include the Primate of Canada, the Archbishop of the West Indies, and the President-Bishop of the Episcopal Church's newest Province, the Anglican Church of the Central American Region.

Bishop of the Episcopal Church of Cuba
The Rt. Rev. Jorge Perera Hurtado
Calle 6, No. 273, Vedado, Havana 4, Cuba
Tel: (53) 07 321 120
Fax: (53) 07 312 436

The Church of England

Members: 26,000,000

Covering all of England, including the Isle of Man and the Channel Islands, the Church is the ancient national Church of the land. Its structures emerged from the missionary work of St. Augustine,

Clergy participate in a liturgy at the Anglican Centre in Spain.

sent from Rome in 597, and from the work of Celtic missionaries in the north. Throughout the Middle Ages, the Church was in Communion with the See of Rome, but in the sixteenth century it separated from Rome and rejected the authority of the Pope. The Church of England is the established Church, with the administration governed by a General Synod that meets twice a year.

Primate of All England and Metropolitan
The Most Rev. and Rt. Hon. George Leonard Carey
  (Archbishop of Canterbury)
Lambeth Palace, London SE1 7JU England
Tel: (44) 0171 928 8282
Fax: (44) 0171 261 9836

Falkland Islands

In 1977, the Archbishop of Canterbury resumed jurisdiction over the Falkland Islands and South Georgia, which had been relinquised in 1974 to the Church of the Southern Cone of America.

The Rector Rev. Alastair McHaffie
The Deanery, Stanley, Falkland Islands, South Atlantic
Fax: (500) 21842

The Church of North India

Members: 1,250,000

The Church was inaugurated in 1970 after many years of preparation. It includes the Anglican Church, the United Church of Northern India (Congregationalist and Presybterian), the Methodist Church (British and Australian Conferences), the Council of Baptist Churches in Northern India, the Church of the Brethren in India, and the Disciples of Christs. Along with the Church of South India, the Church of Pakistan, and the Church of Bangladesh, it is one of the four United Churches.

Moderator and Bishop of Cuttack
The Most Rev. Dhirendra Kumar Mohanty
Bishop's House, Madhusudan Rd., Cuttack 753 001,
   Orissa, India
Tel: (91) 0671 602 016
Fax: (91) 0671 602 206

The Church of South India

Members: 2,000,000

The Church was inaugurated in 1947 by the union of the South India United Church (itself a union of Congregational and Presbyterian/Reformed traditions), the southern Anglican dioceses of the Church of India, Burma, and Ceylon, and the Methodist Church in South India. It is one of the four United Churches in the Anglican Communion.

Moderator and Bishop of Colmbatore
The Most Rev. Dr. Vasant Dandin
Bishop's House, 204 Race Course Rd., Colmbatore 641018,
   TN1, India
Tel: (91) 042 221 3605
Fax: (91) 044 852 3528

The Church of the Province of the Indian Ocean

Members: 90,486

The Province, covering Madagascar, Mauritius, and Seychelles, was founded in 1973, combining two bishoprics. The Anglican mission began in Mauritius in 1810, after the capture of the island from the French. Missionaries were then sent to the other islands.

Archbishop of the Province
The Most Rev. Remi Rabenirina (Bishop of Antananarivo)
Eveche Anglican, Ambohimanoro, 101 Antananarivo,
  Madagascar
Tel: (261) 020 222 0827
Fax: (261) 020 226 1331

The Church of Ireland

Members: 410,000

Tracing its origins to St. Patrick and his companions in the fifth century, the Irish Church has been marked by strong missionary efforts. In 1537, the English king was declared head of the Church, but most Irish Christians maintained loyalty to Rome. The Irish Church Act of 1869 provided that the statutory union between the Churches of England and Ireland be dissolved and that the Church of Ireland should cease to be established by law. A General Synod of the Church, established in 1890 and consisting of Archbishops, Bishops, and representatives of the clergy and laity, have legislative and administrative power.

The Primate of All Ireland and Metropolitan
The Most Rev. Robert Henry Alexander Eames
  (Archbishop of Armagh)
See House, Cathedral Close, Armagh, BT61 7EE,
  Northern Ireland
Tel: (44) 01861 527 155
Fax: (44) 01861 522 851

The Holy Catholic Church in Japan
(Nippon Sei Ko Kai)

Members: 57,273

In 1859, the American Episcopal Church sent two missionaries to Japan, followed some years later by representatives of the Church of England and the Church of Canada. The first Anglican Synod occurred in 1887. The first Japanese Bishops were consecrated in 1923. The Church remained underground during World War II and assumed all Church leadership after the war. *Sei Ko Kai Shumbun,* the Church monthly, is augmented by NSKK, published in English.

Acting Primate of the Holy Catholic Church in Japan
The Rt. Rev. Joseph Noriaki Iida (Bishop of Kyushu)
Provincial Office Nippon Sei Ko Kai, 65 Yarai-cho, Shinjukuku,
    Tokyo 162, Japan
Tel: (81) 03 5528 3171
Fax: (81) 03 5228 3175

The Episcopal Church in Jerusalem and the Middle East

Members: 10,000

The Church covers Jerusalem, Iran, Egypt, Cyprus, and the Gulf. The Jerusalem bishopric was founded in 1841 and became an archbishopric in 1957. Reorganization in January 1976 ended the archbishopric and combined the Diocese of Jordan, Lebanon, and Syria with the Jerusalem bishopric after a nineteen-year separation. Around the same time, the new Diocese of Cyprus and the Gulf was formed and the Diocese of Egypt was revived. The Cathedral Church of St. George the Martyr in Jerusalem is known for its ministry to pilgrims. St. George's College, Jerusalem, is in partnership with the Anglican Communion.

President-Bishop of the Episcopal Church in Jerusalem and the
    Middle East
The Most Rev. Ghais Abd El-Malik (Bishop in Egypt with North
    Africa, Ethiopia, Somalia, Eritrea, and Djibouti)
Diocesan Office, PO Box 87, Zamalek Distribution,
    Cairo, Egypt
Tel: (20) 02 341 4019
Fax: (20) 02 340 8941

The Anglican Church of Kenya

Members: 2,500,000

Mombasa saw the arrival of Anglican missionaries in 1844, with the first Africans ordained to the priesthood in 1885. Mass conversions occurred as early as 1910. The first Kenyan Bishops were consecrated in 1955. The Church became part of the Province of East Africa, established in 1960, but by 1970 Kenya and Tanzania were divided into separate Provinces.

Primate of the Anglican Church of Kenya
The Most Rev. David Gitari (Bishop of Nairobi)
PO Box 40502, Nairobi, Kenya
Tel: (254) 02 714 755
Fax: (254) 02 714 750

The Anglican Church of Korea

Members: 14,558

From the time the Rt. Rev. John C. Corfe arrived in Korea in 1890 until 1965, the Diocese of Korea had English Bishops. In 1993 the Archbishop of Canterbury installed the newly elected Primate and handed jurisdiction to him, making the Anglican Church of Korea a Province of the Anglican Communion. There are four religious communities in the country as well as an Anglican University.

Primate of the Anglican Church of Korea
The Most Rev. Bundo C. H. Kim (Bishop of Pusan)
3 Chong-dong, Chung-ku, Seoul 100-120, Korea
Tel: (82) 02 735 6157
Fax: (82) 02 737 4210

Lusitanian Church
(Portuguese Episcopal Church)

Members: 5,000

The American Episcopal Church organized the Lusitanian Church, Catholic Apostolic Evangelical in 1880. The Church consisted of Roman Catholic Priests who formed congregations in and around Lisbon using a translation of the 1662 English Prayer Book. A Lusitanian Bishop was consecrated in 1958 and in the early 1960s many Provinces of the Anglican Communion established full Communion with the Church in Portugal. Full integration occurred in 1980 when the Church became an extraprovincial diocese under the metropolitical authority of the Archbishop of Canterbury.

Bishop of the Lusitanian Church
The Rt. Rev. Dr. Fernando da Luz Soares, Secretaria Diocesana
Apartado 392, P-4430 Vila Nova de Gaia, Portugal
Tel: (351) 02 375 4018
Fax: (351) 02 375 2016

The Church of the Province of Melanesia

Members: 163,884

After 118 years of missionary association with the Church of the Province of New Zealand, the Church of the Province of Melanesia was formed in 1975. The Province encompasses the Republic of Vanuatu, Solomon Islands, and the French Trust Territory of New Caledonia, both sovereign island nations in the South Pacific.

Archbishop of the Church of the Province of Melanesia
The Most Rev. Ellison L. Pogo (Bishop of Central Melanesia)
Provincial Headquarters, PO Box 19, Honiara, Solomon Islands
Tel: (677) 21 137
Fax: (677) 21 098

The Anglican Church of Mexico

Members: 21,000

The Mexican Episcopal Church symbolically began with Mexico's war for independence in 1810. Religious reform in 1857 secured freedom of religion, separating the Roman Catholic Church from government and politics. In 1860, the newly formed Church of Jesus contacted the Episcopal Church in the United States, seeking leadership, guidance, and support. In 1958, the fourth missionary Bishop of Mexico was the first of the Church's Bishops to be consecrated on Mexican soil. The Church became an autonomous Province of the Anglican Communion in 1995.

Primate
The Most Rev. Samuel Espinoza (Bishop of Western Mexico)
FCO Javier Gambo #255, Col. Sector Juarez, 44100
   Guadalajara, Jal, Mexico
Tel: (52) 03 615 5070
Fax: (52) 03 615 4413

The Church of the Province of Myanmar

Members: 49,257

Anglican chaplains and missionaries worked in Burma in the early and mid-nineteenth century. The Province of Myanmar was formed in 1970, nine years after the declaration of Buddhism as the state religion and four years after all foreign missionaries were forced to leave.

Archbishop of the Province of Myanmar
The Most Rev. Andrew Mya Han (Bishop of Yangon)
40 Pyidaungsu Yeiktha Rd., Dagon PO (11191), Yangon,
   Myanmar
Tel: (95) 01 285 379
Fax: (95) 01 251 405

The Church of the Province of Nigeria

Members: 17,500,000

The rebirth of Christianity began with the arrival of Christian freed slaves in Nigeria in the middle of the nineteenth century. The Church Missionary Society established an evangelistic ministry, particularly in the south. The division of the Province of West Africa in 1979 formed the Province of Nigeria and the Province of West Africa. During the 1990s, nine missionary Bishops consecrated themselves to evangelism in northern Nigeria.

Archbishop of Province I
The Most Rev. Joseph A. Adetiloye (Bishop of Lagos)
Archbishop's Palace, 29 Marina, PO Box 213, Lagos, Nigeria
Tel: (234) 1 263 6026
Fax: (234) 1 263 1264

Archbishop of Province II
The Most Rev. Benjamine Chukuemaka Nwankiti
  (Bishop of Owerri)

Archbishop of Province III
The Most Rev. Peter Jasper Akinola (Bishop of Abuja)

The Church of Pakistan

Members: 800,000

One of four United Churches in the Anglican Communion, the Church of Pakistan was inaugurated in 1970. Members include the Anglican Churches of India, Pakistan, Burma, and Ceylon, two conferences of the United Methodist Church, the United Presbyterian Church in Pakistan, two Church councils, and the Pakistan Lutheran Church.

Moderator and Bishop of Raiwind
The Most Rev. Samuel Azariah
17 Warris Road, PO Box 231, Lahore 3, Pakistan
Tel: (92) 042 758 8950
Fax: (92) 042 757 7255

The Anglican Church of Papua New Guinea

Members: 246,000

Organized as a missionary diocese of Australia in 1898, the Church was part of the Australian Province of Queensland until 1977. The first indigenous priest was ordained in 1914. The Anglican Church functions mostly in rural areas where mountains and rain forest provide natural barriers to travel. Sixty percent of the funding is raised internally; the balance comes from grants from Australia, New Zealand, and the United Kingdom-based Papua New Guinea Church Partnership.

Archbishop of the Anglican Church of Papua New Guinea
The Most Rev. James Ayong (Bishop of Aipo Rongo)
PO Box 893, Mt. Hagen, Western Highlands Province,
  Papua New Guinea
Tel: (675) 52 1131
Fax: (675) 52 1181

Anglicans affirm that God's love extends to people of every culture.
In Southern Africa.

Episcopal Church in the Philippines

Members: 118,187

With its history as a Spanish colony, the Philippines was predominantly Roman Catholic. When Americans colonized the country in 1898, Anglican missionary work began in the north and among Muslim populations in the south. Four dioceses were established by

1971. The Church consecrated its first Bishop in 1963 and became an autonomous Province in 1990.

Prime Bishop of the Episcopal Church in the Philippines
The Most Rev. Ignacio Capuyan Soliba
PO Box 10321, Broadway Centrum, 1112 Quezon City,
   Philippines
Tel: (63) 02 7075 91/2/3/4
Fax: (63) 02 721 19 23

The Church of the Province of Rwanda

Members: 1,000,000

In just over 10,170 square miles are 180,000 Anglicans, out of a quickly growing population of 7.7 million. The former Ruanda Mission established its first station at Gahini in 1925 and grew through the revival of the 1930s and 1940s, with the first Rwandan Bishop appointed in 1965. Eight dioceses have up to 40 parishes, which in turn comprise 15–20 congregations. Like all strata of Rwandan society, the Church suffered through the genocide, and it is a major priority of the church to replace clergy through training. The Church has a role as a healing ministry to the many traumatised people in Rwanda and to reconciliation, restoration, and rehabilitation. The Church has also been involved in rural development, medical work, vocational training, and education.

Archbishop of the Province of Rwanda
The Most Rev. Emmanuel Mbona Kolini (Bishop of Kigali)
BP 61, Kigali, Rwanda
Tel: (250) 76 338
Fax: (250) 73 213

The Scottish Episcopal Church

Members: 53,553

The roots of Scottish Christianity go back to St. Ninian in the fourth century and St. Columba in the sixth. After the Reformation, the Episcopal Church was the established Church of Scotland. It was disestablished and replaced by the Presbyterian Church in 1689. Penal statutes in force from 1746 to 1792 further weakened the Church, yet Bishops maintained continuity. In 1794 in Aberdeen, the Scottish Church consecrated the first Bishop of the American Church. There was rapid growth in the nineteenth century influenced by the Tractarian Movement.

Primus
The Most Rev. Richard Holloway (Bishop of Edinburgh)
21a Grosvenor Crescent, Edinburgh EH12-5EL
Tel: (44) 0131 538 7033
Fax: (44) 0131 538 7088

The Church of the Province of South East Asia

Members: 168,079

The Anglican Church in South East Asia was originally under the jurisdiction of the Bishop of Calcutta, India. The first chaplaincy was formed in West Malaysia in 1805; the first bishop was consecrated in 1855. The Diocese of Labuan, Sarawak, and Singapore was formed in 1881, dividing in 1909, 1962, and 1970. Until the inauguration of the Church of the Province of South East Asia, the four dioceses (Kutching, Sabah, Singapore, and West Malaysia) were under the jurisdiction of the Archbishop of Canterbury. Although the Province exists under the restrictions of a Muslim government, the Church has experienced spiritual renewal and has sent out its own mission partners to various parts of the world.

Primate
The Most Rev. Moses Tay (Bishop of Singapore)
4 Bishopsgate, Singapore 249970
Tel: (65) 474 1661
Fax: (65) 479 5482

The Church of the Province of Southern Africa

Members: 2,000,000

The Province is the oldest in Africa. British Anglicans met for worship in Cape Town after 1806, with the first Bishop appointed in 1847. The twenty-three dioceses of the Province extend beyond the Republic of South Africa and include the Foreign and Commonwealth Office (St. Helena and Tristan da Cunha), Mozambique (Lebombo and Niassa), the Republic of Namibia, the Kingdom of Lesotho, and the Kingdom of Swaziland.

Primate
The Most Rev. Winston Njongonkulu Ndungane
  (Archbishop of Cape Town)
Bishopcourt, Claremont, Cape Province 7700, South Africa
Tel: (27) 021 761 2531/2
Fax: (27) 021 761 4193

The Anglican Church of the Southern Cone of America

Members: 22,490

British immigrants brought Anglicanism to South America during
the nineteenth century. The South American Missionary Society
continues to work among indigenous peoples. In 1974, the Archbishop of Canterbury gave over his metropolitical authority for
the dioceses of the Southern Cone and, in 1981, the new Province
was formed. It includes Argentina, Bolivia, Chile, Paraguay, Peru,
and Uruguay.

The Presiding Bishop
The Most Rev. Maurice Sinclair (Bishop of Northern Argentina)
Casilla de Correo 187, CP 4400 Salta, Argentina
Tel: (54) 087 311 718
Fax: (54) 087 312 622

Spanish Reformed Episcopal Church

Members: 5,000

Under the leadership of a former Roman Catholic Priest, the Spanish Reformed Church was under the pastoral care of the Bishop of
Mexico starting in 1880. In 1894, the Bishop of Meath consecrated
the first Bishop and the Church of Ireland accepted metropolitan
authority. The Church was fully integrated in 1980 as an extraprovincial diocese under the metropolitical authority of the Archbishop of Canterbury.

Bishop
The Rt. Rev. Carlos Lopez-Lozano
Beneficiencia 18, 28004, Madrid, Spain
Tel: (34) 1 445 25 60
Fax: (34) 1 594 45 72

The Church of Sri Lanka

Members: 52,500

Until 1970, the Church was part of the Church of India, Pakistan, Burma, and Ceylon. The first Anglican services were held in 1796, and missionaries began their work in 1818. The Church continues as extraprovincial under the Archbishop of Canterbury.

The Rt. Rev. Kenneth MJ Fernando (Bishop of Colombo)
368/2 Bauddhaloka Mawatha Colombo 7 Sri Lanka
Tel: (94) 01 696 208
Fax: (94) 01 684 811

The Church of the Province of Sudan

Members: 2,000,000

The Church Missionary Society began work in 1899 in Omdurman; Christianity spread rapidly among black Africans of the southern region. Until 1974, the Diocese of Sudan was part of the Jerusalem archbishopric. It reverted to the jurisdiction of the Archbishop of Canterbury until the new Province, consisting of four new dioceses, was established in 1976. Civil and religious strife and a constant flow of refugees have challenged the Church.

Archbishop of the Church of the Province of Sudan
vacant

The Church of the Province of Tanzania

Members: 1,379,366

The Universities Mission to Central Africa and the Church Missionary Society began work in 1864 and 1878 at Mpwapwa. The Province was inaugurated in 1970 following the division of the Province of East Africa into the Province of Kenya and the Province of Tanzania. The sixteen dioceses represent both evangelical and Anglo-Catholic Churches.

Archbishop of the Church of the Province of Tanzania
The Most Rev. Donald L. Mtetemela
Box 1028, Iringa, Tanzania
Tel: (255) 064 2667
Fax: (255) 064 2079

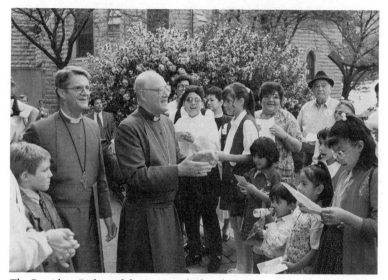

The Presiding Bishop of the Episcopal Church, USA, and the Archbishop of Canterbury visit a congregation in Chicago, Illinois.

The Church of the Province of Uganda

Members: 8,000,000

After its founding in 1877 by the Church Missionary Society, the Church grew through the evangelization of Africans by Africans. The first Ugandan clergy were ordained in 1893 and the Church of Uganda, Rwanda, and Burundi became an independent Province in 1961. The history of the Church in Uganda has been marked by civil strife and martyrdom. In May 1980 the new Province of Burundi, Rwanda, and Zaire was inaugurated; the Province of Uganda has grown since then from seventeen to twenty-seven dioceses.

The Archbishop of the Province of Uganda
The Most Rev. Livingstone Mpalanyi-Nkoyoyo
   (Bishop of Kampala)
PO Box 14124, Kampala, Uganda
Tel: (256) 041 270 218/9
Fax: (256) 041 250 922

The Episcopal Church of the United States of America

Members: 2,400,000

Anglicanism was brought to the New World by explorers and colonists with the first celebration of the Holy Eucharist in Jamestown, Virginia, in 1607. There was no resident Bishop for nearly two hundred years, causing problems when many of the clergy sided with the Crown during the American Revolution. In 1784, the Scottish Episcopal Church consecrated the first American Bishop. The Church maintains ninety-eight dioceses plus twenty overseas jurisdictions.

The Presiding Bishop and Primate
The Most Rev. Frank Tracy Griswold III
815 Second Ave., New York, NY 10017
Tel: (212) 922 5323
Fax: (212) 490 3298

The Church in Wales

Members: 93,721

The Church in Wales was disestablished and partially disendowed in 1914 and 1919. In 1920, the new Province of Wales was created. The Anglican Church is the largest denomination in the country, with its own Board of Missions and two bilingual Church magazines, Y Llan and Welsh Churchman.

Archbishop
The Most Rev. Alwyn Rice Jones (Archbishop of Wales)
(Bishop of St. Asaph)
Esgobty, St. Asaph, Clwyd LL17 OTW, Wales
Tel: (44) 01745 583 503
Fax: (44) 01745 584 301

The Church of the Province of West Africa

Members: 1,000,000

Church work began in Ghana as early as 1752 and in Gambia, Ghana, Guinea, Liberia, and Sierra Leone in the nineteenth century. The Province of West Africa was founded in 1951 and was divided to form the Province of Nigeria and the Province of West Africa in 1979. The Church exists in an atmosphere of civil strife and Christians remain a minority.

Archbishop and Primate
The Most Rev. Robert Okine (Bishop of Koforidua)
PO Box 980, Koforidua, Ghana
Tel: (233) 081 22329
Fax: (233) 21 669 125 (ACCRA)

The Church in the Province of the West Indies

Members: 770,000

The West Indies became a self-governing Province of the worldwide Anglican Communion in 1883 because of the Church of England missions in territories that became British colonies. It is made up of two mainland dioceses and six island dioceses, including Barbados, Belize, Guyana, Jamaica, Nassau and the Bahamas, Tobago, Trinidad, and the Windward Islands. Great emphasis is being placed on training personnel for an indigenous ministry. The island locations and scattered settlements make pastoral care difficult and costly.

Archbishop
The Most Rev. Orland Lindsay (Bishop of North Eastern
   Caribbean and Aruba)
Bishop's Lodge, PO Box 23, St. John's, Antigua, West Indies
Tel: (268) 462 0151
Fax: (268) 462 2090

Life of the Communion

The Faith

The Scripture and the Gospels, the Apostolic Church and the early Church Fathers are the foundation of Anglican faith and worship. The basic tenants, as formulated for the purpose of discussions in Christian Unity, can be found in what is called the Chicago-Lambeth Quadrilateral 1886–1888, and read as follows:

1. Anglicans view the Old and New Testaments "as containing all things necessary for salvation" and as being the rule and ultimate standard of faith.

2. We understand the Apostles' Creed as the baptismal symbol, and the Nicene Creed as the sufficient statement of the Christian faith.

3. The two sacraments ordained by Christ himself—Baptism and the Supper of the Lord—are administered with unfailing use of Christ's words of institution, and the elements are ordained by him.

4. The Historic Episcopate is locally adapted in the methods of its administration to the varying needs of the nations and peoples called of God into the unity of his Church.

Anglicans trace their Christian roots back to the early Church, and their specifically Anglican identity to the post-Reformation expansion of the Church of England and other Episcopal or Anglican Churches. Historically there were two main stages in the development and spread of the Communion. Beginning with the seventeenth century, Anglicanism was established alongside colonialisation in the United States, Australia, Canada, New Zealand, and South Africa. The second stage began in the eighteenth century when missionaries worked to establish Anglican churches in Asia, Africa, and Latin America.

As a worldwide family of churches, the Anglican Communion has more than 70 million adherents in thirty-seven Provinces spreading across 160 countries. Located on every continent, Anglicans speak many languages and come from different races and cultures. Although the Churches are autonomous, they are also uniquely unified through their history, their theology, their worship, and their relationship to the ancient See of Canterbury.

Anglicans uphold the Catholic and Apostolic Faith. Following the teachings of Jesus Christ, the Churches are committed to the proclamation of the good news of the Gospel to the whole creation. Faith and practice are based on the revelation contained in Holy Scripture and the Catholic Creeds, and is interpreted in light of Christian tradition, scholarship, reason, and experience.

By baptism in the name of the Father, Son, and Holy Spirit, a person is made one with Christ and received into the fellowship of the Church. This sacrament of initiation is open to children as well as to adults.

Central to worship for Anglicans is the celebration of the Holy Eucharist, also called the Holy Communion, the Lord's Supper, the Mass. In this offering of prayer and praise, the life, death, and resurrection of Jesus Christ are recalled through the proclamation of the word and the celebration of the sacrament. Other important rites, commonly called sacraments, include Confirmation, Holy Orders, Reconciliation, Marriage, and Anointing of the Sick.

Worship is at the very heart of Anglicanism. Its styles vary from simple to elaborate, from evangelical to Catholic, from charismatic to traditional, or even a combination of these various traditions. The Book of Common Prayer, in its various revisions throughout the Communion, and additional liturgical studies give expression to the comprehensiveness found within the Church whose principles reflect that of the *via media* in relation to its own and other Christian Churches.

The Archbishop of Canterbury

The Archbishop of Canterbury fills a unique position in the worldwide Anglican Communion. As *Primus Inter Pares,* First Among Equals, of the Bishops, he serves the Anglican Church as spiritual leader. As Archbishop of Canterbury, he also calls Anglicans together for various meetings. He meets with his fellow Bishops for the Lambeth Conference once a decade. A meeting of the Primates, the Archbishop or most senior Bishop for each Church, occurs every two to three years. The Archbishop of Canterbury also meets representatives from every Church in all orders—Bishop, Priest, Deacon, Laity—at the Anglican Consultative Council. These three bodies, plus the office of the Archbishop himself, form the instruments of unity. These meetings throughout the Communion provide a forum for discussion, consultation, and mutual support for the Church's membership, while honouring the autonomy and interdependence of each of the Churches.

Another part of the Archbishop's job is an ecumenical one. Anglicans believe that they are part of the One Holy Catholic and Apostolic Church. They are members of the World Council of Churches and are in dialogue with most Christian bodies, in particular the Roman Catholics, the Lutherans, the Methodists, the Reformed Churches, the Orthodox Churches, and the Oriental Orthodox

The Secretary General meets the Holy Father.

Churches. The Archbishop of Canterbury, as a world Church leader, has a particular role to play in his relationship with such leaders.

In addition to the important roles the Archbishop takes on for the ministry of the Anglican Communion, he also is the Bishop of Canterbury in England, and Archbishop of the Province of Canterbury, which includes the Diocese of Central and Southern England and the Diocese in Europe. The Archbishop of Canterbury is Primate of All England. He also has a seat in the House of Lords, and thus, an important voice in the British Parliament. In addition to these, he has special authority over a small number of dioceses around the world that are not yet autonomous, having not attained provincial status.

The Primates Meeting and the Anglican Consultative Council

At the 1978 Lambeth Conference of Bishops, the then Archbishop of Canterbury, Dr. Donald Coggan, proposed that the Archbishop or Senior Bishop in each Province (commonly called the Primates), should meet reasonably often for "leisurely thought, prayer and deep consultation." Lord Coggan saw these meetings as an opportunity to provide a place for real exchange of "mind, will and heart." As the Communion had grown, and the number of dioceses had increased, the Lambeth Conference had become a very large gathering. The Primates Meeting therefore provided a very important way for the Communion to keep in touch on a more frequent and practical basis. Since 1979, the Primates of the Provinces of the Communion's Churches have met every two or three years to consult on theological, social, and international issues. In recent years they have been joined by the Moderators of the Churches of India, Pakistan, and Bangladesh.

Some Anglicans would like the Primates to have specific authority on particular issues, while others argue that all authority must lie in each individual Anglican Province. This is an age-old tension within the Church. Anglican Churches, however, rely heavily on the leadership role of their Bishops, those consecrated to serve the diocesan family as witnesses to the resurrection. Churches are usually governed by a synod or convention that includes Bishops, clergy, and laity. Indeed most structures of the Anglican Communion are far from rigid and have been adapted and changed to suit the need of the Church at a particular time.

Key to understanding the ecclesiology of Anglican Christianity is examining the work of what is called the Anglican Consultative Council. This is a designated group of men and women, lay and ordained, young and old, from every corner of the globe, who meet every two to three years to discuss matters of vital concern to the member Provinces, as well as to the whole Communion. The Council was formed after the 1968 Lambeth Conference. The Bishops saw a need for a more frequent and more representative contact among the churches than was possible through their once-a-decade conference of Bishops. The President of the Council is the Archbishop of Canterbury, and the ongoing work is overseen by a chairperson and a vice-chairperson, and with regular meetings of an elected standing committee.

The Lambeth Conference

Every Anglican diocese and now, beginning with the 1998 Conference, all active Bishops of the Anglican Communion attend the Lambeth Conference. The Conference gathers under the presidency of the Archbishop of Canterbury to discuss the major issues and concerns that face the Church. Though not technically binding, the resolutions of the Lambeth Conference are significant and are noted with great care by the Churches of the Communion, and by the religious and secular world as well.

The first Lambeth Conference was held in 1867. It brought together seventy-six Bishops and was presided over by Archbishop Charles Longley. The Conference of 1908 was preceded by a large pan-Anglican Conference that included seven thousand lay and clerical deputies. The 1920 Conference was important for its "appeal to all Christian people, for reunion," and this message was sent to the heads of all Christian communities throughout the world. The issues of unity and ecumenical relations have since been central to every Lambeth Conference. Since 1968 the Conferences have also included a number of observers and participants from other Christian bodies, as well as Anglican consultants who were not Bishops.

Due to the increasing number of Bishops and the growth of the Church, the Lambeth Conference moved from its original meeting place, Lambeth Palace, and met at Church House in 1968. In 1978 it moved again, this time to the University of Kent, where subsequent Conferences have been held. The 1998 Conference will host more than eight hundred Bishops from nearly six hundred dioceses. It also welcomes full membership to the Anglican Consultative Council. The first Lambeth Conferences were dominated by English-speaking Europeans reflecting the leadership of the Anglican Communion at that time. By 1988 twice the number of African Bishops attended Lambeth than were present in 1978.

The importance of the Lambeth Conferences to the Communion as a whole was emphasized in the final address to the Lambeth Conference of the then Archbishop of Canterbury, Dr. Robert Runcie. The Bishops, he said, had been repeatedly reminded of the obligations of their common life: "Common life—that is what we have experienced here, a common life which lies at the heart of the Communion. Our Communion here has not been a quiet blending together, like sleepy little streams trickling into some big pool. It has been the vigorous meeting of persons with both their ideas and hopes and passions." The Archbishop concluded by saying "Humility, generosity and adventurous Christianity—these are the things you will take from this Conference back to your diocese where I pray you will dare to do great things for God."

The Anglican Communion Office and Secretariat

A small staff based in London at the Anglican Communion Office assists the Anglican Consultative Council, the Primates Meeting, the Lambeth Conference, and the Archbishop of Canterbury with his international tasks. The office is headed by the Secretary General of the Anglican Communion, the Reverend Canon John L. Peterson. There is also an Executive Assistant to the Secretary General, and Executive Officers for Ecumenical Affairs, Finance and Administration, Communication, Telecommunication, and Evangelisation Resources.

Communication is essential to the unity and work of the Anglican Communion, and the Secretariat works diligently in gathering, receiving, and editing news from around the Communion. It distributes this news throughout the Communion in a variety of ways. A weekly Anglican Communion News Service appears on the Internet, and telecommunications is generally used to provide urgent news that must be transmitted immediately around the Anglican Communion. Because not all parts of the Communion are able to enjoy the luxury of telecommunication, the Secretariat also prepares written information and sends it by the fastest possible means to the Provinces. The Secretariat is also responsible for a number of publications. It cooperates with the compilation of the *Anglican Cycle of Prayer* and the magazine *Anglican World,* a quarterly which contains features, news, and photographs from around the Communion. An increasing number of reports, leaflets, and books are being produced by the communications office as well.

The Secretariat is funded by the Inter-Anglican budget, with contributions coming from the member Churches, Provinces of the Anglican Communion, according to their membership statistics and financial means.

The Personal Emergencies' Fund

The Anglican Communion, and in particular the Anglican Consultative Council, is not a fund-raising or donor agency, but it is called to meet emergencies from time to time and is constantly being asked to assist various ministries throughout the Communion. A small but important fund has been established—the Personal Emergencies' Fund—to meet particular emergency needs that are not funded by other sources. The particular purpose of such a fund is to assist in personal cases of Bishops, Clergy and Lay Workers, their families or dependents where there is some urgent or critical need. This may arise out of the circumstances of their work or as a result of external circumstances. All applications are processed through the local Bishop's office. The fund is supported by voluntary donations from the Provinces, Member Churches, private individuals, and other Anglican bodies. The accounts of the Personal Emergencies' Fund are kept as part of the Anglican Communion Office administration.

Finance and Administration

The bonds of affection in the Anglican Communion are very strong. Often divisive issues test the strength of our family unity, but indeed, as years succeed to years, the realization that we have a Gospel to proclaim is foremost in the thinking of our leadership around the world. Our interdependence indicates that we clearly want to and need to stay together. Any family needs to talk with one another; to share responsibilities, joys, and sorrows; and to relate to neighbours if it is to develop in harmony and service to the world around it, and to the world that God has given it to minister to in this age. As far as a family of Churches is concerned, this cannot happen without adequate funding. Thus, face-to-face communication, such as that made possible by the Anglican Consultative Council, the Primates Meetings, and the Lambeth Conference, as well as by the visits of the Archbishop, is a costly venture.

Key to the success of these meetings is the ability to be adaptable to the changing needs of the Church, as well as the maintenance of a speedy and efficient system of communications. Where there is good communication, there is compassion. Sharing responsibilities in mission, evangelism, and pastoral care involves structures for

The Archbishop regularly hosts ecumenical leaders in Canterbury.

policy making and neutral transfer of resources. Relating to our fellow Christians in the ecumenical role requires bilateral and multilateral conversations in which Anglicans need to speak as a single body. All these activities require servicing by the Anglican Communion Secretariat, a relatively small staff drawn from different countries, and this must be accompanied by an adequate budget. The goal of the Secretariat is to increase the awareness level of the ministries that the Anglican Communion provides worldwide. It is also hoped that through good communication we can share resources and experiences from global north to global south, north to north, south to south, and east to west and west to east. We hope the reality of our family, the global family of Anglicanism, will move us from a state of being comfortable to being committed and confident that we do have a message to proclaim to a broken world, and that we do need to share the grace, love, and peace that comes from God and the salvation that comes to us all through Jesus Christ. Thus the budget-making process for the Anglican Communion must carry conviction, and the administration create confidence. Generally speaking, the core budget is far from meeting the demands that are being increasingly made on the Secretary General and his staff in London. This is cause for deep concern as communications improve and the global nature of our church becomes more and more of a reality that is shared on every level of church life, and most importantly on the level of the local congregation.

The Inter-Anglican Finance Committee is in command of looking at available funding and how each of the Provinces is assessed in its giving to the work of the Communion. Once an Inter-Anglican budget is formulated, the amount needed to carry out the ministry authorised is divided up among the Provinces of the Communion in accordance with the formula agreed to by the Anglican Consultative Council. These percentages are designed to ensure that every member Church of the Anglican Communion shares in the budget process. Allocations are calculated, taking into account the number of members in each church and the relative affluence of the location of the church.

Networks

Throughout the Anglican Communion there are a number of special networks. These groupings consist of people who have a particular interest, expertise, or concern that they wish to highlight to the wider Anglican Communion. The work of the network is done in cooperation with the Anglican Communion Office staff. Current networks include the Peace and Justice Network, the Family Network, a Youth Network, a Refugee Network, a Women's Network, and the Inter Faith Network. These networks are expected to be self-funding, though the Secretariat assists, wherever possible, their work.

Liturgy

Within Anglicanism that is rooted in the tradition of the Book of Common Prayer, there is a tremendous diversity of worship and ceremonial ritual vestments, and of traditional and indigenous music. In recent years there also have been considerable changes in many provincial prayer books and alternate service books. Key to understanding this process is the work of the Inter-Anglican Liturgical Consultation.

The Compass Rose Logo

The Compass Rose, a symbol identifying those who belong to the worldwide Anglican Communion, is used worldwide and is the logo of the Anglican Communion Secretariat in London.

The emblem of the Anglican Communion, the Compass Rose, was originally designed by the late Canon Edward West of New York. The modern design is that of Giles Bloomfield. The symbol, set in the nave of the mother church of the Anglican Communion, Cathedral Church of Christ in Canterbury, was dedicated by Archbishop of Canterbury Robert Runcie at the final Eucharist of the Lambeth Conference in 1988.

Lord Runcie dedicated a similar Compass Rose in Washington Cathedral in 1990, further encouraging its worldwide use. The emblem also has been incorporated into an official Anglican Communion flag created by the Reverend Bruce Nutter of Australia.

The centre contains the cross of St. George, reminding Anglicans of their origins. The Greek inscription "The truth shall make you free," which surrounds the cross, recalls the spread of Anglican Christianity throughout the world. The mitre at the top emphasises the role of the Episcopacy and Anglican Order that is at the core of the traditions of the Churches of the Communion.

The Compass Rose Flower

(from The Anglican Digest)
A new rose variety, bred by the Notcutts, was launched at the 1997 Chelsea Flower Show by the Archbishop of Canterbury in anticipation of the Lambeth Conference 1998. Held every ten years, Lambeth

Launched at the Chelsea Flower Show in 1997, the Compass Rose serves as a beautiful symbol of the life of the Anglican Communion.

is the gathering of Bishops of the worldwide Anglican Communion at Canterbury under the presidency of the Archbishop.

The idea that a special rose be developed and grown for the Anglican Communion was that of Mrs. Roger Symon, who oversees the fifty-member Canterbury Cathedral flower guild, which is responsible for the flowers in the Cathedral.

Inspired by the emblem of the Anglican Communion, the Compass Rose is a truly beautiful and highly scented shrub rose that won the Henry Edland Memorial Medal for the best-scented rose, and a Trial Ground Certificate of the Royal National Rose Society, St. Alban's, 1995.

The rose has been planted at Canterbury and at Lambeth Palace, and will be available for bishops to take home with them from Lambeth in 1998. It can be planted globally as a living reminder of the Anglican family of churches.

Mrs. Eileen Carey, who has been instrumental in this project, said, "The Compass Rose is a symbol of the planting, growth, and flowering of Anglicanism around the world. It bears both the thorns of suffering that so many have experienced for their faith and the beautiful bloom that has opened to mark their achievement in the great rose we now behold."

The Leadership of George Carey

George Leonard Carey was born on November 13, 1935 in Bow in the East End of London. His father worked as a hospital porter, and George was the oldest of five children. He completed his secondary education at Bifrons Secondary Modern School in Barking, leaving school at fifteen.

He was first employed as an office boy with the London Electricity Board, going on at eighteen to do his National Service in the Royal Air Force. Afterward he returned to the Electricity Board, but had already decided to seek ordination. He studied intensely to gain a place at King's College, University of London and the London College of Divinity. He graduated with a degree in divinity (BD) in 1962 and was ordained deacon in the same year.

Anglican officials prepare for Lambeth.

Dr. Carey spent four years in his first curacy at St. Mary's, Islington in North London. He continued to study and was awarded a Master of Theology degree (MTh) for a thesis on "Church, Ministry, Eucharist in the Apostolic Fathers." From Islington he went to the staff of Oak Hill Theological College as a lecturer in theology in 1966, moving to St. John's College, Nottingham in 1970, where he also served as chaplain. During these years he obtained a further degree (PhD) for a thesis on second-century ecclesiology.

From 1975 to 1982, Dr. Carey was vicar of St. Nicholas' Church, Durham where he led the church forward in a program of expansion and renewal. He described this period in his book *The Church in the Market Place*. In addition to his parochial activities, he acted as a prison chaplain at a Youth Custody prison. He also maintained his links with the RAF, serving as chaplain to the Durham branch of the RAF Association.

In 1982 he was appointed Principle of Trinity College, Bristol, and saw the college through a time of change and growth. During his five years in Bristol he served as an elected member of the Church of England's General Synod and was appointed a member of the Board for Mission and Unity, and has served as chairman of its Faith and Order Advisory Group.

Dr. Carey is the author of eight books on theological issues on topics including chistology, ecumenism, relationships with the Roman Catholic Church, and the existence of God. He has also contributed articles and reviews to many journals and periodicals.

Dr. Carey became Bishop of Bath and Wells early in 1988. Once in office, he introduced and conducted a series of teaching missions, seeking to deepen faith and knowledge in deaneries and parishes.

Eileen Carey is a daughter of Scottish parents (Mr. and Mrs. Douglas Cunningham Hood) who moved to Dagenham shortly before the war. Mrs. Carey was born there and was educated at South East County Technical College in Barking, Essex. On leaving school she completed a qualification in nursing at West London Hospital. She later worked at Mount Vernon Hospital, Northwood in the Radio Therapy Unit. In recent years she has worked part-time in several nursing homes. She married Dr. Carey in 1960 and they have four adult children (two sons and two daughters) and two grandchildren.

Archbishops of Canterbury

SEQUENCE	NAME	CREATED
1	Augustine (consecrated Bp 597)	601
2	Lauréntius	604
3	Mellitus	619
4	Justus	624
5	Honorius	627
6	Deusdsdit	655
7	Theodorus	668
8	Beorhtweald	692
9	Tatwine	731
10	Nothelm	735
11	Cuthbeorht	740
12	Breguwine	761
13	Jaenbeorht	765
14	Asthelheard	793
15	Wulfred	805
16	Feologild	832
17	Ceolnoth	833
18	Aethelred	870
19	Plegmund	890
20	Aethelhelm	914
21	Wulfhelm	923
22	Oda	942
23	Aelfsige	959
24	Beorhthelm	959
25	Dustan	959
26	Aethelgar	988
27	Sigeric Serio	990
28	Aelfric	995
29	Aelfheah	1005
30	Lyfing	1013
31	Aethelnoth	1020
32	Eadsige	1038
33	Robert (Champart) of Jumieges	1051
34	Stigand	1052
35	Lanfranc	1070
36	Anselm	1093

SEQUENCE	NAME	CREATED
37	Ralph d'Escures	1114
38	William de Corbeil	1123
39	Theobald	1138
40	Thomas à Becket	1162
41	Richard (of Dover)	1174
42	Baldwin	1185
43	Hubert Walter	1193
44	Stephen Langton	1207
45	Richard le Grant (of Wetharshed)	1229
46	Edmund Rich	1234
47	Boniface of Savoy	1245
48	Robert Kilwardby	1273
49	John Pecham (Peckham)	1279
50	Robert Winchelsea	1294
51	Walter Reynolds	1313
52	Simon Mepeham	1328
53	John de Stratford	1333
54	Thomas Bradwardine	1349
55	Simon Islip	1349
56	Simon Langham	1366
57	William Whittlesey	1368
58	Simon of Sudbury	1375
59	William Courtenay	1381
60	Thomas Arundel	1396
61	Roger Walden	1398
	Thomas Arundel (restored)	1399
62	Henry Chicheley	1414
63	John Stafford	1443
64	John Kemp	1452
65	Thomas Bourchier	1454
66	John Morton	1486
67	Henry Dean	1501
68	William Warham	1503
69	Thomas Cranmer	1533
70	Reginald Pole	1556
71	Matthew Parker	1559
72	Edmund Grindal	1576
73	John Whitgift	1583

SEQUENCE	NAME	CREATED
74	Richard Bancroft	1604
75	George Abbot	1611
76	William Laud	1633
77	William Juxon	1660
78	Robert Sheldon	1663
79	William Sancroft	1678
80	John Tillotson	1691
81	Thomas Tenison	1695
82	William Wake	1716
83	John Potter	1737
84	Thomas Herring	1747
85	Matthew Hutton	1757
86	Thomas Secker	1758
87	Frederick Cornwallis	1768
88	John Moore	1783
89	Charles Manners-Sutton	1805
90	William Howley	1828
91	John Bird Sumner	1848
92	Charles Thomas Longley	1862
93	Archibald Campbell Tait	1868
94	Edward White Benson	1883
95	Frederick Temple	1896
96	Randall Thomas Davidson	1903
97	Cosmo Gordon Lang	1928
98	William Temple	1942
99	Geoffrey Francis Fisher	1945
100	Arthur Michael Ramsey	1961
101	Frederick Donald Coggan	1974
102	Robert A. K. Runcie	1980
103	George Leonard Carey	1991

Anglicans at the United Nations

The Anglican Communion has a unique ministry to the United Nations in New York City: focusing on those who are suffering social, political, and economic injustices. Thus it plays a key role in actively working to affirm the dignity and well-being of all 70 million members of the Anglican family in 160 countries around the world.

The Anglican Office at the United Nations plays a humanitarian role at the United Nations, bringing biblical and theological perspectives into dialogues involving spiritual leaders, heads of governments, and leaders of major international and nongovernmental organisations. It seeks to influence the global dialogue, decision making, and actions at the United Nations, particularly in the areas of human rights, the environment, gender issues, international debt, disarmament, and our ability to guise and assist in diplomatic efforts.

It also facilitates the delivery of the vast resources of the United Nations to the people of the Anglican Communion by working with the United Nations' 184 member states, 12 social service agencies, and 2,500 nongovernment organisations (NGOs) around the world. In doing so, it assists the United Nations in implementing the goal of its charter: "to promote social progress and better standards of life in larger freedom."

The Anglican Office at the United Nations is not totally part of the Anglican Communion core budget, but it is underwritten by contributions from individual people and institutions.

The Gathering at Lambeth

Seventy-six bishops attended the first Lambeth Conference in 1867.

Lambeth Conference: The Hope

An address by the Reverend Canon Andrew Deuchar,
The Archbishop of Canterbury's Secretary for
Anglican Communion Affairs at Lambeth Palace,
to a gathering of Lambeth Degree Holders
at St. Matthew's Church, Westminster, 1997

I am not sure how the short straw was parcelled out on this occasion, but somehow it has ended up in my hands to try offering you some reflections on the forthcoming Lambeth Conference. Last week, when I saw the list of those who would be presenting today, I tried to engineer a good dose of flu, or an emergency trip to Norfolk Island, because I quickly realised that a significant number of people in this room would have far more experience and personal knowledge of the hopes invested in the Conference than I have—which is not difficult since I have none (except, I suppose, for an idea of some of the hopes of the present Archbishop of Canterbury).

Then, as I thought about the title I ended up with—which, by the way, I chose, so I have no one else to blame—I further realised that it was actually a hopeless task. How could I, a relatively inexperienced, English non-Bishop, even begin to present to you what the hopes of 850 Bishops from every corner of the globe (if globes have corners) might be. These Bishops have seen families, friends, and colleagues hacked to death in Rwanda; they have lived and ministered in the most extraordinary situations of isolation and anti-Christian cultures—in Iran and Burma and Pakistan. I could go on, but you do not need me to rehearse each and every situation that actually isolates me from the normal life of so many in our Communion, and therefore the hopes and expectations for this unique gathering we know as the Lambeth Conference. But I can hazard a few guesses, and my first (I hope an informed one) is that the subject that will not be at the top of many of their agendas is sex.

But let me go back a bit. Let me first offer someone else's view of what actually is the Lambeth Conference. In their introduction to their report of the 1988 Conference, entitled *Lambeth: A View from the Two Thirds World* (SPCK, 1989), Vinay Samuel and Chris Sugden offer this description:

> The Lambeth Conference is the most comprehensive and perhaps the most comprehensible expression of the Global Anglican Communion. For in its membership and meetings, its strengths and its weaknesses, its unity and diversity, it dramatically pictures the nature of the Communion. It provides a once-in-ten-years opportunity to survey the life of the Communion in its totality, as given through the experiences and opinions of its global order of senior leaders, it diocesan bishops.

Well, apart from that last point—the 1998 Conference will include suffragan and assistant Bishops who are in full-time diocesan appointments—I think that gives a clear picture of what actually it is all about. Of course, such a description would be unlikely to appear in any official publicity, nor, I suspect, would very many individual Bishops express their hopes for the Conference in quite these terms. But the reality is that this is an accurate description: "In its membership and meetings, its strengths and its weaknesses, its unity and diversity, it dramatically pictures the nature of the Communion."

Of course, whether you have 76 Bishops meeting in the Guard Room at Lambeth Palace, as at the first Conference in 1867, or 850 Bishops overrunning (if Bishops run) the campus of the University of Kent, the hopes and expectations that come with them will be widely, not to say wildly, open. So what might they be? Well, rather than simply guess at that, I have tried, for the purposes of this afternoon, to trawl some views—not really from the Bishops of today, but rather from some of those of the past. The interesting thing to try to judge is the extent to which the hopes expressed fifty or a hundred years ago remain relevant to the Anglican Communion today.

The first Lambeth Conference of 1867 was called together, of course, because of crises in the colonies. Bishop Colenso of Natal had been let loose upon the Church and excommunicated by the Bishop of Cape Town, and those well-known conservatives in

Canada were perturbed by the effect of these events on the rest of the Church. The provincial synod decided to urge the Archbishop of Canterbury to provide a means

> by which members of our Anglican Communion in all quarters of the world should have a share in the deliberations of her welfare, and be permitted to have a representation in one General Council of her members gathered from every land. Deeply affected by the threat of isolation which recent declarations in high places have indicated, we earnestly solicit this measure, as maintaining that test of communion which is to us the most precious.

There are, I think, a number of resonances with life in the Church today—the need for deliberation, a sense of isolation, not least from "those in high places," and the sense of the preciousness of the common life and traditions of the Communion. Interesting that even now, with thirty-six Provinces and every modern means of communication, the isolation still appears to be present.

Archbishop Longley's final assent to call together the Bishops of the Home and Colonial Episcopate contains this warning:

> Such a meeting would not be competent to make declarations or lay down definitions on point of doctrine. But united worship and common counsels would greatly tend to maintain practically the unity of faith; whilst they would bind us together in straiter bonds of peace and brotherly charity (from *The Lambeth Conferences of 1867, 1876 and 1888*, edited by Randall T. Davidson, SPCK, 1896).

Thus, in almost classical words, are set out the hopes of successive archbishops, and I know that the present Archbishop would certainly be associated with such hopes. Deliberations, discussions, arguments, certainly—that is the nature of the Church and of human beings—but in the corporate worship of the Conference lies the heart not just of the Conference itself, but of the whole Communion. Joined together as one, with eyes and hearts set on God, in penitence, praise, and thanksgiving is what communion is. And it is for this reason that Dr. Carey takes such a strong stand on Communion, and the dangers inherent in breaking that Communion. Communion does not mean agreement on this doctrine or that moral teaching; it means that in this person or that person I recognise a sister or brother in Christ who has, like me, been loved and redeemed. That is a powerful message that is fundamental to Anglicanism, perhaps uniquely among the Churches of the world, and to which the Lambeth Conference will bear powerful witness—I hope!

Of course, today, very few people would understand the fuss Bishop Colenso caused, although the way the case was handled by the Bishop of Cape Town and in the passages of the establishment here would still, I suspect, raise a few eyebrows of disestablishmentarians. Still, it is probably too much to hope for that Bishops will arrive into the future with the perspective of a century as they tackle some of the issues that divide us.

I suspect, however, that there will be more than a few Bishops arriving in Canterbury who will be less than enthusiastic about Archbishop Longley's definition. The common worship is OK, although it seems there might even be a threat to that from one or two quarters. When one Primate talks about deciding who is in Communion with him and his Church, that represents something of a threat to a common eucharistic celebration. But there surely will be some who expect some defining documents that have more authority and that function as more than simple consultation documents.

The Lambeth Conference has a good record in providing significant theological papers and, on occasion, good transforming initiatives. The year 1988, of course, saw the unexpected launch of the Decade of Evangelism, which, despite cynicism from some quarters, has been enthusiastically marked in many parts of the Communion. The 1920 Conference produced one of the most significant pieces of work in the early twentieth century, the Appeal to All Christian People, and the 1958 Conference produced the report *The Family in Contemporary Society,* which I recall using in my theological training in 1983, and which Adrian Hastings rates "amongst the ablest statements to come from any authoritative Church body in the twentieth century." He goes on to say, "The Bishops of the Anglican Communion were speaking at this point from both a maturely developed formal moral theology and with the benefit of personal experience" (from *A History of English Christianity 1920 to 1985,* Fount, 1987).

But despite Hastings's use of the word "authoritative," these documents were and are not binding upon the Communion. Some are beginning to say that in order to hold the Communion today, we must have some system of defining Anglican teaching, at least in the fundamentals. Well, it will be interesting to see whether or not anyone can reach agreement on what the fundamentals are, let alone what should be the content thereof.

But this pressure is not new, nor, I suggest, are the issues potentially more explosive for us today than were those that faced the Church in 1878, for instance, in the context of the new intellectual challenge to belief and the simmering rows between the various parties of the Church. It was no one less than the great Dr. Pusey who wrote to Archbishop Tait a few weeks before that Conference opened:

> You are going to preside, my dearest Archbishop, over a band of men who have been called to an Apostolic burden of authority . . . We can expect, and we do expect with confidence, that God the Holy Spirit will guide your deliberations, and what you say will come to us with the Lord's own stamp upon it, and we, your children, will receive and obey the message you deliver to us.

What archbishop today could fail to be seduced by such a touching promise of submission! And there will certainly be those who hope for an authoritative statement on sexuality, on the use of the Bible, on land mines, on the war in Bougainville, and on whaling in Canada. It is inevitable that some hopes will be dashed, and it is one of the Archbishop's hopes that Conference resolutions will be kept to an absolute minimum. There is always a danger that a conference such as this dares not to be seen as silent on an issue of concern to its members, and thus rushes into a resolution that has not been sufficiently worked at and researched. I am sure that all "old hands" here will be able to identify examples of that.

What we do hope for, however, and this I believe is a common hope across the Communion, is a very significant contribution to the debate on international debt, an issue that is threatening to destroy human society in many countries, especially in Africa. We have the ability to bring together real experience of the deprivations that people are suffering with people who really understand the difficulties faced by the creditors in dealing with the issue. Watch this space.

We also hope that in the Virginia Report—a report from the Inter-Anglican Theological and Doctrinal Commission on the instruments of unity in the Communion (which is technically a report to the Lambeth Conference, although it has already been published)—we have a really substantial document of Anglican ecclesiology that will serve the Communion well as we explore how we may more effectively become a Communion of Churches, rather than a collection of autonomous Provinces. Already it has been warmly welcomed by the Anglican-Roman Catholic International Commission and the Patriarchate of Constantinople.

But that mention of the pressure to speak, to pronounce, leads me to another area that concerns us all, and that seems to dominate more and more: the influence of the media. It is from the media that the real pressure will come to talk about issues in public that we would rather not. From the media will come the pressure to identify individual Bishops who can stir up controversy, and I suppose amongst 850 it is inevitable that there will be a few who will seek out opportunities to do so. It is the media that will try to make the Conference dance to its tune. It was so in 1988, when the ordination of women, especially as Bishops, was pushed as the issue, as were also the general attacks on the Communion and the Archbishop of Canterbury. Peter Davis, of the Communications team from New Zealand, was quoted as saying:

> The Conference was like a ship being tossed on a heavy sea. Gunboats gathered, helicopters gathered, periscopes popped up. The British press had arrived. . . . It developed like a cartoon of the mind. In a helicopter above the vessel, a photographer called out, "Could you head for the rocks? We'd prefer an action photograph!"

There is no doubt what the media will be hoping for—a huge, terminal row over sexuality issues. Our hope is rather different, and this takes me back to where I began. Our hope is that there will be mature, open, and honest debate on issues that matter; that even when there is profound disagreement, as there will be, our Communion in the living Christ will strengthen the bonds of friendship. But even more important will be those heroes of our Communion whose lives and livelihoods are constantly under threat, that they will return encouraged and strengthened and rested as a result of being among brothers and sisters in Christ, and fellow pilgrims on the Way.

Resolutions of
the Twelve Lambeth Conferences

Although not a legislative meeting, the Lambeth Conference has an important influence on the life of the Churches of the Anglican Communion. Resolutions passed at previous Lambeth Conferences show that a wide variety of topics and concerns are discussed. Here is a list of sample resolutions from the various Conferences since the first Lambeth Conference in 1867.

Resolutions passed by a Lambeth Conference are then normally ratified by the individual Provinces of the Anglican Communion as needed and as desires dictate. A resolution from the Lambeth Conference is not binding on the Anglican Communion as a whole, but expresses the mind of the gathering of Bishops and is held in high respect.

1867 Resolution 8

That, in order to the binding of the Churches of our colonial empire and the missionary Churches beyond them in the closest union with the Mother-Church, it is necessary that they receive and maintain without alterations the standards of faith and doctrine as now in use in that Church. That, nevertheless, each Province should have the right to make such adaptations and additions to the services of the Church as its peculiar circumstances may require. Provided, that no change or addition be made inconsistent with the spirit and principles of the Book of Common Prayer, and that all such changes be liable to revision by any synod of the Anglican Communion in which the said Provinces shall be represented.

1888 Resolution 10

That, inasmuch as the Book of Common Prayer is not the possession of one diocese or Province, but of all, and that a revision of one portion of the Anglican Communion must therefore be extensively felt, this Conference is of the opinion that no particular portion of he Church should undertake revision without seriously considering the possible effect of such action on other branches of the Church.

1897 Resolution 19

That it is important that, so far as possible, the Church should be adapted to local circumstances, and the people brought to feel in all ways that no burdens in the way of foreign customs are laid upon them, and that nothing is required of them but what is of the essence of faith, and belongs to the due order of the Catholic Church.

1908 Resolution 20

All races and peoples, whatever their language or conditions, must be wielded into one body, and the organisation of different races living side by side into separate or independent Churches, on the basis of race or colour, is inconsistent with the vital and essential principle of the unity of Christ's Church.

1920 Resolution 15

The Conference urges on every branch of the Anglican Communion that it should prepare its members for taking part in the universal fellowship of the reunited Church, by setting before them the loyalty which they owe to the universal Church, and the charity and understanding which are required of the members of so inclusive a society.

1930 Resolution 49

The Conference approves the following statement of the nature of the status of the Anglican Communion, as that term is used in its Resolutions:

The Anglican Communion is a fellowship, within the one Holy Catholic and Apostolic Church, of those duly constituted dioceses, Provinces, or regional Churches in communion with the See of Canterbury, which have the following characteristics in common:

they uphold and propagate the Catholic and Apostolic faith and order as they are generally set forth in the Book of Common Prayer as authorised in their several Churches; they are particular or national Churches, and, as such, promote within each of their territories a national expression of Christian faith, life and worship; and

they are bound together not by a central legislative and executive authority, but by a mutual loyalty sustained through the common counsel of the Bishops in conference.

Anglicans express the unchanging Gospel of Christ in words, actions, and customs that communicate with relevancy in local contemporary society. In Bermuda.

The Conference makes this statement praying for and eagerly awaiting the time when the Churches of the present Anglican Communion will enter into communion with other parts of the Catholic Church not definable as Anglican in the above sense, as a step towards the ultimate reunion of all Christendom in one visibly united fellowship.

**1948 Resolution 51—Thankfulness for
Growing Unity**

The Conference records its thankfulness to Almighty God for the revival of interest in the cause of Christian unity which has been increasingly manifested in many parts of the world. It also pays a tribute of gratitude to all those in our own and in other Communions who have displayed courage, enterprise, and vision in the service of this cause.

1958 Resolution 65—Movement of Peoples

The Conference emphasises the importance of the witness for Christ which can be borne when Christians go from one country to another, especially to countries where Christians are a small minority, and urges that ways and means be developed to assist both clergy and members of the laity to do so effectively. It also urges that every effort be made, especially on the parochial level, to practise Christian fellowship with people of other nations and races who come to live permanently in a new land.

1958 Resolutions on the Bible

1. The Conference affirms its belief that the Bible discloses the truths about the relation of God and man which are key to the world's predicament and is therefore deeply relevant to the modern world.

2. The Conference confirms that our Lord Jesus Christ is God's final word to man, and that in his light all Holy Scripture must be seen and interpreted, the Old Testament in terms of promise and the New Testament in terms of fulfillment.

3. The Conference affirms that Jesus Christ lives in his Church through the Holy Spirit according to his promise, and that the Church is therefore both guardian and interpreter of Holy Scripture; nevertheless the Church may teach nothing as "necessary for eternal salvation but what may be concluded and proved by the Scripture."

4. The Conference welcomes every sign of the revival of Bible study within the common life of the Church. It calls on all Church people to reestablish the habit of Bible reading at home, and commends the growing practice of group Bible study.

5. The Conference acknowledges gratefully the work of scientists in increasing man's knowledge of the universe, wherein is seen the majesty of God in his creative activity. It therefore calls upon Christian people both to learn reverently from every new disclosure of truth, and at the same to time bear witness to the biblical message of a God and Saviour apart from whom no gift can be rightly used.

6. The Conference welcomes the new translations of Scriptures in many languages, and would encourage our people to give all possible support to those societies whose concern is the distribution of the Scriptures to all lands. Much still remains to be done in this field and the need is urgent.

1958 Resolutions of the Commemoration of Saints and Heroes of the Christian Church in the Anglican Communion

Resolution 77

The Conference holds that the purpose of a Kalendar is to increase our thankfulness to God and to strengthen our faith by recalling regularly the great truths of the Gospel, the principal events in the life of our Lord, and the lives and examples of men and women who have borne preeminent witness to the Holy Spirit, and are with us in the communion of saints.

Resolution 78

The Conference considers that the power to revise or amend Kalendars should be exercised by the same authority as is required for the revision of the Book of Common Prayer within each several Church or province, which authority may allow supplementary commemorations for local use in addition to the Kalendar at the request of a diocese.

Resolution 79

The Conference is of the opinion that the following principles should guide the selection of saints and heroes for commemoration:

(a) In the case of scriptural saints, care should be taken to commemorate men or women in terms which are in strict accord with the facts made known in the Holy Scripture.

(b) In the case of other names, the Kalendar should be limited to those whose historical character and devotion are beyond doubt.

(c) In the choice of new names, economy should be observed and controversial names should not be inserted until they can be seen in the perspective of history.

(d) The addition of a new name should normally result from a widespread desire expressed in the region concerns over a reasonable period of time.

Resolution 80

The Conference recommends that the Church should continue to commemorate the saints in three ways: by Red Letter days, Black Letter days, or a memorial collect alone.

1968 Resolution 10—Consultation Regarding World Peace

The Conference invites the Archbishop of Canterbury on its behalf to consult with the Pope and the Oecumenical Patriarch and the Praesidium of the World Council of Churches in the possibility of approaching leaders of the other world religions with a view to convening a conference at which in concert they would speak in the interests of humanity on behalf of world peace.

1978 Resolution 8—The Church's Ministry of Healing

The Conference praises God for the renewal of the ministry of healing within the Churches in recent times and reaffirms

that the healing of the sick in his name is as much a part of the proclamation of the kingdom as the preaching of the good news of Jesus Christ;

that to neglect this aspect of ministry is to diminish our part in Christ's total redemptive activity;

that the ministry to the sick should be an essential element in any revision of the liturgy (see the *Report of the Lambeth Conference of 1958*, p. 2.92).

1978 Resolution 12—Anglican Conferences, Councils, and Meetings

The Conference asks the Archbishop of Canterbury, as President of the Lambeth Conference and President of the Anglican Consultative Council, with all the Primates of the Anglican Communion, within one year to initiate consideration of the way to relate together the international conferences, councils, and meetings within the Anglican Communion so that the Anglican Communion may best serve God within the context of one, holy, Catholic, and Apostolic Church.

1988 Resolution 22—Christ and Culture

This conference:

Recognises that culture is the context in which people find their identity.

Affirms that God's love extends to people of every culture and that the Gospel judges every culture according to the Gospel's own criteria of truth, challenging some aspects of culture while endorsing and transforming others for the benefit of the Church and society.

Urges the Church everywhere to work at expressing the unchanging Gospel of Christ in words, actions, names, customs, liturgies, which communicate relevantly in each contemporary society.

Elements of Faith

Anglican worship is based on the principle that God's will for the world has been made known in Jesus Christ. At Walsingham.

What Anglicans Believe
David L. Edwards, D.D.

Anglican worship had been "corporate" or "common" (together) but structured. Thomas Cranmer, Archbishop of Canterbury, edited the Book of Common Prayer—one of the noblest books in the English language. Issued in 1549, it was able to speak to the heart, yet almost all the time maintained the highest standards of beauty. Changes were later made. Another prayer book was issued for Scotland in 1637 that influenced the first American prayer book (1789).

In recent years almost all the Anglican Churches in the world have issued more modern services, since the language of 1549 and 1637 is no longer always understood. Many of these services have provided greater freedom than Cranmer thought proper, so that contemporary hopes and concerns can be voiced. Another great enrichment has come through the increasing use of hymns—some of them now old and very famous, but some new and experimental. And along with the hymns there has also been the development of music for the choir and the organ.

This worship is dominated by the Bible. For hundreds of years churchgoers loved to hear the magnificent English of the Psalms (the Old Testament's hymns), as translated by Bishop Miles Coverdale in 1535, and the lessons from the Authorised Version of the Bible, issued in 1611 (during Shakespeare's lifetime). Then modern translations became necessary. Still, however, the principle remains: Our common prayer is best when together we have heard the word of God through the Scriptures, the writings gathered in the Bible. Anglicans sit under the Bible.

Anglican 'doctrine' or teaching is therefore based on the Bible. American Anglican Churches share with the Church of England on essential points of doctrine, discipline, and worship. An official definition, adopted in 1973, states: "The doctrine of the

Church of England is grounded in the Holy Scriptures, and in such teachings of the ancient Fathers and Councils of the Church as are agreeable to the said Scriptures. In particular such doctrine is found in the Thirty-nine Articles of Religion, the Book of Common Prayer, and the Ordinal." The Articles of Religion mentioned in that definition is a document, last revised in 1572, that

In corporate worship, believers unite in acknowledging the holiness of God. In Hong Kong.

states the Church of England's position in the theological contro-versies of the time. The Ordinal is the collection of services for "ordaining" or setting aside the clergy.

This does not mean that the Anglican life is confined to what was explicitly laid down in the Bible or in the ancient Church or in the Tudor Age. No! Anglicanism has been a living experience, changing as faithful Christians have changed. Successive genera-tions, and very different groups and individuals, have added to the riches of Anglican worship and to the vigour of Anglican life.

In Anglicanism, laypeople matter. They do not exist to support the clergy; instead the clergy exist to support the laypeople. The mission of the Church is not mainly in the hands of the clergy; it depends on laypeople as they live and work at a distance from any church building. In Anglican committees, councils, or synods (conferences with power), laypeople sit, discuss, and vote along-side the clergy. In the congregation, the neighbourhood, or the nation, the church is very much bigger than the clergy.

Since the eighteenth century Anglican laypeople have been encouraged to think for themselves and have been free to do so without fear or heresyhunts. They have been left free to form their own opinions, to make their own decisions, to take their own ini-tiatives, without having to consult the clergy at every point. Priests have also been encouraged to be scholars and thinkers with the freedom needed to seek truth and express it. The teachers of the Church have been men and women educated alongside laypeople, familiar with contemporary thoughts, and often teaching and writ-ing in the universities. And the Church has been heavily involved in education at every level.

This involvement in the life of society has brought great prob-lems. For example, there has been the problem of the relation between religion and politics, which has led to many controversies. Most members of the Church are nervous about "mixing religion and politics" and are particularly suspicious of priests who "get mixed up in politics." This is understandable. Christianity has a message that goes far deeper than any political programme could ever do, and the Church should not be identified with any political party. But there ought to be some connection between religion and politics. Religion should inspire us with the vision of God's love for humanity. Politics ought to drive us into loving action to help those in need—according to our own consciences, not to any dictation by clergy. Christians ought, therefore, to express their love by active service, whether they do this by taking a particular political role or by quietly trying to help those around them.

Some famous Anglican thinkers have disturbed the complacent by preaching a vision of a society founded on brotherhood and justice. The best way of honouring great Anglican tradition is to carry on the batter for a better society in our own day. Not all Anglicans are heroic enough, but at least they do know where the Church stands and where their duty lies on many issues. For example, the Church is thick in the fight against racial prejudice and the colour bar. The Anglican leadership in this fight in South Africa has been brave and has won worldwide respect. The recent history of the Episcopal Church in the United States has contained many examples of courageous action in the course of social justice.

Problems of a very different sort have been raised by the work of the scholars on the Bible and on the traditions of the Church. Anglican scholars, possessing so much freedom, have often reached critical conclusions. These have often challenged the orthodoxy of less critical members of the Church. Such problems have led to fierce controversies, but in these—as in debates of political matter—the view of the Church as a whole has not been finally expressed by any Bishop or any other leader. The mind of the Church has been made known gradually, as a result of free thought and free speech.

It is sometimes suggested that Anglicanism is a mere debating society, composed of individuals who are so "liberal" that they agree on nothing. But Anglicanism has in it strong Evangelical and Catholic elements, reminding it that it exists in order to be obedient to Jesus Christ.

The Evangelical (or "Low Church") movement in Anglicanism safeguards the insistence of the Protestant Reformation on the right and the duty of each person to make his or her own decision to be reconciled to God through Jesus Christ. There is great emphasis on the fact that redemption from sin is the free gift of God, not earned by any good that a person may do but given to those who, in simple trust, accept Jesus Christ as Saviour and Lord. With this goes a great emphasis on the privilege and duty of personal Bible study. Worship is simple, making clear that what matters is the response to the message in the Bible. And resulting from this, there is great emphasis on evangelism—spreading the good news of Jesus Christ.

Anglican Evangelicals have been suspected of sentimentality, but they have often been marked by enthusiasm and attractiveness in daily life, for their Bible-based religion has been warmly personal. Evangelicalism was revived during the eighteenth century—at a time when most of the rest of Anglican life had grown cold because of a dull emphasis on being moderate, reasonable, and respectable. In the twentienth century, Evangelicalism is being revived again, and again it is meeting a spiritual need.

The Catholic (or "High Church") movement in Anglicanism safeguards the continuity within the Church before the Reformation, but at the same time does not accept the claims of the Popes or many customs that are regarded as corruptions of the early form of Catholicism.

Anglo-Catholicism tends to have more elaborate services and stresses the traditions of the Church. It was strong during the seventeenth century as a reaction against the Puritanism of Oliver Cromwell and the like. It revived during the nineteenth century, in what was known as the Oxford Movement, as a reaction against compromise with the materialism of modern society. It has restored much of the old beauty to churches and church services, and it has restored the old insistence on personal holiness through self-discipline. The Anglican communities of monks and nuns have been examples to many.

Anglo-Catholicism has often been suspected as an attempt to take people back to the religion of the Middle Ages. But whatever our opinions may be about details, the Catholic movement in Anglicanism is not a separate religion. On the contrary, Anglicanism is loyal to what the great majority of Christians have believed and done in the Catholic Church since the beginning.

Anglicanism accepts and devoutly uses the two sacraments founded by Jesus Christ himself: Baptism and Holy Communion. A sacrament has been described as "the use of material things as signs and pledges of God's grace, and as a means by which we receive his gifts." For example, the use of water in baptism is a sign of God's saving goodness, and a means of receiving it.

Anglicanism also accepts and devoutly repeats the two creeds that have their roots in the days before the Church was divided.

One is the Apostles' Creed. It was not written by the apostles, but it began in the teaching given to the candidates for baptism in Rome and elsewhere. The word "apostle" means "envoy," and this creed states briefly what was thought to be essential in the message that the apostles passed on to the Church. The other creed is the Nicene Creed, which is from the Council of the Church held in 325 in Nicea. (Some words have been added since this time.) It states briefly what was thought to be most important in the Church's faith: Jesus was both truly human and truly divine. Another, longer document, the Athanasian Creed, is also printed in many prayer books, although nowadays it is seldom used. The majestic hymn "We Praise Thee, O God" (Te Deum laudamus in Latin), written around 400, is often sung or said in Anglican worship, and is creedal in nature.

Essentially what Anglicans do when they use these creeds or sing the Te Deum is state that they are glad to stand in the tradition of faith that the creeds have expressed for so long. They are the heirs of the ages, proud to belong to the brotherhood of the baptized.

Anglicanism also accepts and honours the threefold ministry of Bishops, Priests, and Deacons. The system of having Bishops as leaders is known as Episcopacy. Bishops have been the main leaders of the Church since the second century, and in many ways they carry on the work of the apostles. A Bishop is the spiritual parent to the clergy and the people in a particular area—a diocese. The Bishop is also a teacher of the Christian and Catholic faith, and a planner and inspirator of evangelism and further advance. "Priest" is the shortened form of the word "presbyter" or elder. Priests preside at the Holy Communion, lead local congregations, try to reach all who need their help, and assure sinners of God's forgiveness and healing. "Deacon" is from a Greek word meaning "servant"; Deacons have a special ministry to serve the poor and the sick.

The threefold ministry of Bishop, Priest and Deacon is based on the Catholic way of ordaining them—through prayer and the laying on of hands by a Bishop. At the consecration of a new Bishop, a minimum of three other Bishops must lay on hands in prayer. There is no evidence that in the first centuries of Christianity the Popes of Rome were treated as they came to be treated in the Middle Ages, and as they have been treated by modern Roman Catholics. But there is plenty of evidence that from those early times the work of Catholic Bishops, Priests, and Deacons has been of great importance. And although the Reformation in the sixteenth century caused many controversies about the nature of the ordained ministry and about the nature of Christianity itself, there is plenty of evidence that these controversies are dying down nowadays.

The Catechism

The following is a sample of the many excellent catechisms found in Prayer Books throughout the Anglican Communion. This comprehensive catechism comes from the Church of the Province of Southern Africa.

Human Nature

1. *What are we by nature?*
   We are part of God's creation, made in the image of God.

2. *What does it mean to be created in the image of God?*
   It means that we are free to make choices: to love, to create, to reason, and to live in harmony with creation and with God.

3. *Why then do we live apart from God and out of harmony with creation?*
   From the beginning, humans have misused their freedom and made wrong choices.

4. *Why do we not use our freedom as we should?*
   We rebel against God and put ourselves in the place of God.

5. *What help is there for us?*
   Our help is in God.

6. *How did God first help us?*
   God first helped us by revealing himself and his will through nature and history, through many seers and saints, and especially through the prophets of Israel.

God the Father

7. *What do we learn about God as creator from the revelation to Israel?*
   We learn that there is one God, the Father almighty, creator of heaven and earth, of all that is seen and unseen.

8. *What does this mean?*
It means that the universe is good, that it is the work of a single, loving God who creates, sustains, and directs it.

9. *What does this mean about our place in the universe?*
It means that the world belongs to its creator, and that we are called to enjoy it and care for it in accordance with God's purposes.

10. *What does this mean about human life?*
It means that all people are worthy of respect and honour because all are created in the image of God, and all can respond to the love of God.

On Good Friday, special remembrance is made of the suffering of Jesus on the cross.

11. *How was this revelation handed down to us?*
This revelation was handed down to us from a community created by a covenant with God.

The Old Covenant

12. *What is meant by a covenant with God?*
A covenant is a relationship initiated by God to which a body of people respond in faith.

13. *What is the old covenant?*
The old covenant is the one given by God to the Hebrew people.

14. *What did God promise them?*
God promised them that they would be his people and bring all the nations of the world to him.

15. *What response did God require from the chosen people?*
God required the chosen people to be faithful, to do justice, to love mercy, and to walk humbly with their God.

16. *Where is this old covenant to be found?*
The covenant with the Hebrew people is to be found in the books that compose the Old Testament.

17. *Where in the Old Testament is God's will for us shown most clearly?*
God's will for us is shown most clearly in the Ten Commandments.

The Ten Commandments

18. *What are the Ten Commandments?*
The Ten Commandments are the laws given to Moses and the people of Israel.

19. *Recite the Ten Commandments.*
   I. You shall have no other gods before me.
   II. You shall not make yourself a graven image, or any likeness of anything that is in heaven above, or that is in the earth beneath, or that is in the water under the earth.
   III. You shall not take the name of the Lord your God in vain.
   IV. Remember the Sabbath day, to keep it holy.

V.   Honour your father and your mother.
VI.   You shall not kill.
VII.   You shall not commit adultery.
VIII. You shall not steal.
IX.   You shall not bear false witness against your neighbor.
X.   You shall not covet.

20. *What do we learn from these commandments?*
We learn two things: our duty to God and our duty to our neighbors.

21. *What is our duty to God?*
Our duty is to believe and trust in God:
I.   To love and obey God and to bring others to know him;
II.   To put nothing in the place of God;
III.   To show God respect in thought, word, and deed;
IV.   To set aside regular times for worship, prayer, and the study of God's ways.

22. *What is our duty to our neighbors?*
V.   To love, honour, and help our parents and family; to honour those in authority, and to meet the just demands;
VI.   To show respect for the life God has given us; to work and pray for peace; to bear no malice, prejudice, or hatred in our hearts; and to be kind to all creatures of God;
VII.   To use all our bodily desires as God intended;
VIII. To be honest and fair in our dealings; to seek justice, freedom, and the necessities of life for all people; and to use our talents and possessions as ones who must answer for them to God;
XI.   To speak the truth, and not to mislead others by our silence;
X.   To resist temptations of envy, greed, and jealousy; to rejoice in other people's gifts and graces; and to do our duty for the love of God, who has called us into fellowship with him.

23. *What is the purpose of the Ten Commandments?*
The Ten Commandments were given to define our relationship with God and our neighbors.

24. *Since we do not fully obey the Ten Commandments, are they useful at all?*

Since we do not fully obey them, we see more clearly our sin and our need for redemption.

Sin and Redemption

25. *What is sin?*
Sin is the seeking of our own will instead of God's, thus distorting our relationship with God, other people, and all creation.

26. *How does sin have power over us?*
Sin has power over us because we lose our liberty when our relationship with God is distorted.

27. *What is redemption?*
Redemption is the act of God that sets us free from the power of evil, sin, and death.

28. *How did God prepare us for redemption?*
God sent the prophets to call him back to himself, to show us our need for redemption, and to announce the coming of the Messiah.

29. *What is meant by Messiah?*
The Messiah is the one God sent to free us from the power of sin, so that with the help of God we may live in harmony with God, ourselves, our neighbors, and all creation.

30. *Who do we believe is the Messiah?*
The Messiah, or Christ, is Jesus of Nazareth, the only Son of God.

God the Son

31. *What do we mean when we say that Jesus is the only Son of God?*
We mean that Jesus is the only perfect image of the Father, and he shows us the nature of God.

32. *What is the nature of God revealed in Jesus?*
God is love.

33. *What do we mean when we say that Jesus was conceived by the Holy Spirit and became incarnate from the Virgin Mary?*
We mean that by God's own act his divine Son received our human nature from the Virgin Mary, his mother.

34. *Why did Jesus take on our human nature?*
    The divine Son became human so that in him human beings might be adopted as children of God and be made heirs of God's kingdom.

35. *What is the great importance of Jesus' suffering and death?*
    By his obedience, even to suffering and death, Jesus made the offering that we could not make; in him we are freed from the power of sin and reconciled to God.

36. *What is the significance of Jesus' resurrection?*
    By his resurrection Jesus overcame death and opened for us the way to eternal life.

37. *What do we mean when we say that he descended to the dead?*
    We mean that he went to the departed and offered them also the benefits of redemption.

38. *What do we mean when we say that he ascended into heaven and is seated at the right hand of the Father?*
    We mean that Jesus took our human nature into heaven where he now reigns with the Father and intercedes for us.

39. *How can we share in his victory over sin, suffering, and death?*
    We share in his victory when we are baptized into the new covenant and become living members of Christ.

The New Covenant

40. *What is the new covenant?*
    The new covenant is the relationship with God given by Jesus Christ, the Messiah, to the apostles, and through them, to all who believe in him.

41. *What did the Messiah promise in the new covenant?*
    Christ promised to bring us into the kingdom of God and give us life in all its fullness.

42. *What response did Christ require?*
    Christ commanded us to believe in him and to keep his commandments.

43. *What are the commandments taught by Christ?*
    Christ taught us the summary of the law and gave us the new commandment.

44. *What is the summary of the law?*
    You shall love the Lord your God with all your heart, with all your soul, and with all your mind. This is the first and the greatest commandment. The second is like it: You shall love your neighbor as yourself.

45. *What is the new commandment?*
    The new commandment is that we love one another as Christ loved us.

46. *Where may we find what Christians believe about Christ?*
    What Christians believe about Christ is found in the Scriptures and summed up in the creeds.

The Creeds

47. *What are the creeds?*
    The creeds are statements of our basic beliefs about God.

48. *How many creeds does this Church use in its worship?*
    This Church uses two creeds: the Apostles' Creed and the Nicene Creed.

49. *What is the Apostles' Creed?*
    The Apostle's Creed is the ancient creed of baptism; it is used in the church's daily worship to recall our baptism covenant.

50. *Recite the Apostles' Creed.*
    I believe in God, the Father almighty, creator of heaven and
      earth.
    I believe in Jesus Christ, his only Son, our Lord.
    He was conceived by the Holy Spirit
    and born of the Virgin Mary.
    He suffered under Pontius Pilate
    was crucified, died, and was buried.
    He descended to the dead.
    On the third day he rose again.
    He ascended into heaven
    and is seated at the right hand of the Father.
    He will come again to judge the living and the dead.

    I believe in the Holy Spirit
    the holy Catholic Church

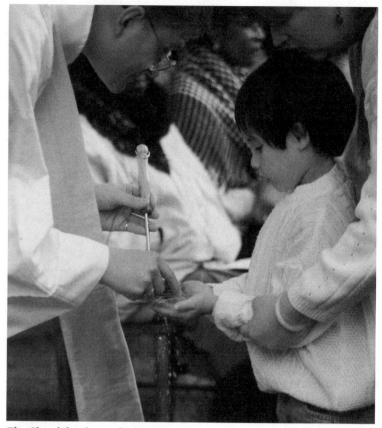

The Church has been a living experience, with successive generations adding to the richness of Anglican life.

    the communion of saints
    the forgiveness of sins
    the resurrection of the body
    and the life everlasting. Amen.

51. *What is the Nicene Creed?*
    The Nicene Creed is the creed of the universal church and is used at the Eucharist.

52. *What is the Athanasian Creed?*
    The Athanasian Creed is an ancient document proclaiming the nature of the Incarnation and of God as Trinity.

53. *What do we mean when speaking of God as Trinity?*
We mean that we believe in God the Father, God the Son, and God the Holy Spirit—three persons and yet one God.

God the Holy Spirit

54. *Who is the Holy Spirit?*
The Holy Spirit is the third person of the Trinity, God at work in the world and in the church even now.

55. *How is the Holy Spirit revealed in the old covenant?*
The Holy Spirit is revealed in the old covenant as the giver of life, the One who spoke through the prophets.

56. *How is the Holy Spirit revealed in the new covenant?*
The Holy Spirit is revealed as the Lord who leads us into all truth and enables us to grow in the likeness of Christ.

57. *How do we recognize the presence of the Holy Spirit in our lives?*
We recognize the presence of the Holy Spirit when we confess Jesus Christ as Lord and are brought into love and harmony with God, ourselves, our neighbors, and all creation.

58. *How do we recognize the truths taught by the Holy Spirit?*
We recognize truths to be taught by the Holy Spirit when they are in accord with the Scriptures.

The Holy Scriptures

59. *What are the Holy Scriptures?*
The Holy Scriptures, commonly called the Bible, are the books of the Old and New Testaments; other books, called the Apocrypha, are often included in the Bible.

60. *What is the Old Testament?*
The Old Testament consists of books written by the people of the old covenant, under the inspiration of the Holy Spirit, to show God at work in nature and in history.

61. *What is the New Testament?*
The New Testament consists of books written by the people of the new covenant, under the inspiration of the Holy Spirit, to set forth the life and teachings of Jesus and to proclaim the good news of the kingdom for all people.

62. *What is the Apocrypha?*
The Apocrypha is a collection of additional books written by the people of the old covenant and used in the Christian Church.

63. *Why do we call the Holy Scriptures the word of God?*
We call them the word of God because God inspired their human authors and because God still speaks to us through the Bible.

64. *How do we understand the meaning of the Bible?*
We understand the meaning of the Bible by the help of the Holy Spirit, who guides the Church in the true interpretation of the Scriptures.

The Church

65. *What is the Church?*
The Church is the community of the Bible.

66. *How is the Church described in the Bible?*
The Church is described as the body of which Jesus Christ is the head and of which all baptized persons are members. It is called the people of God, the new Israel, a holy nation, a royal priesthood, and the pillar and ground of truth.

67. *How is the Church described in the creeds?*
The Church is described as one, holy, Catholic, and Apostolic.

68. *Why is the Church described as one?*
The church is decribed as one because it is one body under one head, our Lord Jesus Christ.

69. *Why is the Church described as holy?*
The church is holy because the Holy Spirit dwells in it, consecrates its members, and guides them to do God's work.

70. *Why is the Church described as Catholic?*
The Church is Catholic because it proclaims the whole faith to all people, to the end of time.

71. *Why is the Church described as Apostolic?*
The Church is Apostolic because it continues in the teaching and fellowship of the apostles and is sent to carry out Christ's mission to all people.

72. *What is the Anglican Communion?*
   The Anglican Communion is a family of churches within the universal Church of Christ that maintains apostolic doctrine and order, and is in full communion with one another and with the See of Canterbury.

73. *What is the Church of the Province of Southern Africa?*
   The Church of the Province of South Africa is a self-governing Province of the Anglican Communion. It proclaims and holds fast the doctrine of the one, holy, Catholic, and Apostolic Church.

74. *What is the mission of the Church?*
   The mission of the Church is to restore all people to unity with God and with each other in Christ.

75. *How does the Church pursue its mission?*
   The Church pursues its mission as it prays and worships, proclaims the Gospel, and promotes justice, peace, and love.

76. *Through whom does the Church carry out its mission?*
   The Church carries out its mission through the ministry of all its members.

The Ministry

77. *Who are the ministers of the Church?*
   The ministers of the church are laypersons, Bishops, Priests, and Deacons.

78. *What is the ministry of laity?*
   The ministry of laypersons is to represent Christ and his Church; to bear witness to him wherever they may be; to carry on Christ's work of reconciliation in the world according to the gifts given to them; and to take their place in the life, worship, and governance of the Church.

79. *What is the ministry of a Bishop?*
   The ministry of a Bishop is to represent Christ and his Church, particularly as apostle, chief Priest, and pastor of a diocese; to guard the faith, unity, and discipline of the whole Church; to proclaim the word of God; to act in Christ's name for reconciliation of the world and the building up of the Church; and to ordain others to continue Christ's ministry.

80. *What is the ministry of a Priest?*

The ministry of a Priest is to represent Christ and his Church, particularly as pastor to the people; to share with the Bishop in the overseeing of the Church; to proclaim the Gospel; to administer the sacrament; and to bless and declare pardon in the name of God.

81. *What is the ministry of a Deacon?*

The ministry of a Deacon is to represent Christ and his Church, particularly as a servant of those in need; and to assist Bishops and Priests in the proclamation of the Gospel and in the administration of the sacraments.

82. *What is the duty of all Christians?*

The duty of all Christians is to follow Christ; to come together week by week for corporate worship; and to work, pray, and give for the spread of the kingdom of God.

The Bishops of the Church of the Province of Southern Africa describe the duty of all Anglican Christians of our Church as thus: The Father expects all his people to witness the Lord Jesus Christ, and in the power of the Holy Spirit to bring others to a knowledge of him.

The Anglican Church in Southern Africa shares in this call, and every baptized and confirmed member must share in God's mission to the world.

To this end, your lifestyle as a Christian should include these responses to God's love for you:

- Come to God in personal prayer every day
- Read the Bible daily
- Receive Holy Communion frequently and in expectant faith
- Follow the example of Jesus in daily life
- Speak about Jesus openly as the Lord whom you know
- Work for justice and reconciliation
- Uphold Christian standards in marriage
- Bring up children to love and serve the Lord
- Give money for God's work and consider the claims of tithing
- Give personal service to the Church and to your neighbor
- Let your life be marked with self-denial and simplicity

Stewardship

83. *What is Christian stewardship?*
Christian stewardship is the way in which Christians exercise their duty to administer what God had entrusted to them and to serve him gladly in his Church.

84. *What has God entrusted to human beings to administer?*
God has entrusted to human beings material possessions, time, and talents, and he has made us stewards of his creation.

Prayer and Worship

85. *What is prayer?*
Prayer is responding to God, by thought and by deeds, with or without words.

86. *What is Christian prayer?*
Christian prayer is response to God the Father, through Jesus Christ, in the power of the Holy Spirit.

87. *What prayer did Christ teach us?*
Our Lord gave us an example of prayer, which is known as the Lord's Prayer.

88. *Recite the Lord's Prayer.*
Our Father in heaven,
hallowed be your name,
your kingdom come,
your work will be done
on earth as it is in heaven.
Give us today our daily bread.
Forgive us our sins,
as we forgive those who sin against us.
Save us from the time of trial,
and deliver us from evil.
For the kingdom, the power, and the glory are yours, now and
forever. Amen.

89. *What are the principle kinds of prayer?*
The principle kinds of prayer are adoration, praise, thanksgiving, penitence, oblation, intercession, petition, meditation, and contemplation.

90. *What is adoration?*
    Adoration is the lifting up of the heart and mind to God, asking for nothing but to enjoy God's presence.

91. *Why do we praise God?*
    We praise God not to obtain anything, but because God's being draws praise from us.

92. *For what do we offer thanksgiving?*
    Thanksgiving is offered to God for all the blessings of this life, for our redemption, and for whatever draws us closer to God.

93. *What is penitence?*
    In penitence we confess our sins and make restitution where possible, with intention to mend our lives.

94. *What is prayer of oblation?*
    Oblation is an offering of ourselves, our lives and labors, in union with Christ for the purposes of God.

95. *What are intercession and petition?*
    Intercession brings before God the needs of others; in petition we present our own needs, that God's will may be done.

96. *What is corporate worship?*
    In corporate worship we unite ourselves with others to acknowledge the holiness of God, to hear God's word, to offer prayer, and to celebrate the sacraments.

97. *What is meditation?*
    Meditation is a form of prayer in which we reflect on a portion of Scripture, or some truth or experience, and ponder it in our hearts.

98. *What is contemplation?*
    Contemplation is a form of prayer in which we keep our hearts and minds still and attentive to God, allowing him to work in us as he will.

Fasting

99. *What is fasting?*
    Fasting is a voluntary act of denying oneself food for a certain length of time.

100. *Why do Christians fast?*
Fasting is a means of self-denial, repentance, intercession, and identification with the needy, and a way of listening to what God has to tell his people.

101. *Why is fasting often associated with prayer?*
Our Lord's example and other scriptural sources teach us that this form of self-discipline is an aid to prayer.

102. *What is abstinence?*
Abstinence is a voluntary act of lessening the quantity of food one eats or denying oneself other pleasures.

103. *When do Christians fast?*
Provincial Synod enacted the following:

DAYS OF FASTING AND SELF-DENIAL

Fast Days
Ash Wednesday and Good Friday are fast days, when the amount of food eaten is reduced.

Days of Self-denial
The weekdays of Lent are days of self-denial.

Other Fridays of the year except:
• Christmas Day
• Fridays following Christmas, Easter, and Ascension Day
• Public holidays falling on a Friday

On these days remembrance is made of the suffering and death of our Lord.

They may be observed in one or more of these ways:
1. By giving more time to prayer, Bible study, or spiritual reading;
2. By eating less or simpler food;
3. By giving up some pleasure or luxury, and using the money saved to help other people.

(Act of Provincial Synod)

Many Christians keep a fast at other times as well in response to a call from their Bishop. Christians also fast at yet other times, such as before receiving Holy Communion or on Fridays.

The Sacraments

104. *What are the sacraments?*

    The sacraments are outward and visible signs of inward and spiritual grace, given by Christ as sure and certain means by which we receive that grace.

105. *What is grace?* ˇ

    Grace is God's favor towards us, unearned and undeserving; by grace God forgives our sins, enlightens our minds, stirs our hearts, and strengthens our wills.

106. *What are the two great sacraments of the Gospel?*

    The two great sacraments given by Christ to his Church are baptism and the Holy Eucharist.

Baptism

107. *What is baptism?*

    Baptism is the sacrament by which God adopts us a his children and makes us members of Christ's body, the Church, and inheritors of the kingdom of God.

108. *What is the outward and visible sign in baptism?*

    The outward and visible sign in baptism is water, in which a person is baptized in the name of the Father, and of the Son, and of the Holy Spirit.

109. *What is the inward and spiritual grace in baptism?*

    The inward and spiritual grace in baptism is union with Christ in his death and resurrection, birth into God's family (the Church), forgiveness of sins, and new life in the Holy Spirit.

110. *What is required of us at baptism?*

    It is required that we renounce Satan, repent of our sins, and accept Jesus as our Lord and Savior.

111. *Why then are infants baptized?*

    Infants are baptized so that they can share citizenship in the covenant, membership in Christ, and redemption by God.

112. *How are the promises for infants made and carried out?*

    Promises are made for them by their parents and sponsors, who guarantee that the infants will be brought up within the Church, to know Christ and be able to follow him.

In the sacramental rite of Confirmation, Anglicans express a mature commitment to Christ.

The Holy Eucharist

113. *What is the Holy Eucharist?*

The Holy Eucharist is the sacrament commanded by Christ for the continual remembrance of his life, death, and resurrection, until his coming again.

114. *Why is the Eucharist called a sacrifice?*

The Eucharist, the Church's sacrifice of praise and thanksgiving, is the way by which the sacrifice of Christ is made present, and in which he unites us to the offering of himself.

115. *By what other names is this service known.*
    The Holy Eucharist is called the Lord's Supper and Holy Communion; it is also known as the Divine Liturgy, the Mass, and the Great Offering.

116. *What are the outward and visible signs in the Eucharist?*
    The outward and visible signs in the Eucharist are bread and wine, given and received according to Christ's command.

117. *What are the inward and spiritual graces in the Eucharist?*
    The inward and spiritual graces in the Holy Communion are the body and blood of Christ given to his people, and received by faith.

118. *What are the benefits we receive in the Lord's Supper?*
    The benefits we receive are forgiveness of our sins, the strengthening of our union with Christ and one another, and the foretaste of the heavenly banquet that is our nourishment in eternal life.

119. *What is required of us when we come to the Eucharist?*
    It is required that we should examine our lives, repent of our sins, and be in love and charity with all people.

Other Sacramental Rites

120. *What other sacramental rites evolved in the Church under the guidance of the Holy Spirit?*
    Other sacramental rites that evolved in the Church include Confirmation, Ordination, Christian Marriage, Confession and Absolution, and the Anointing of the Sick.

121. *How do they differ from the two sacraments of the Gospel?*
    Although they are means of grace, they are not necessary for all persons in the same way that baptism and the Eucharist are.

122. *What is Confirmation?*
    Confirmation is the rite by which we express a mature commitment to Christ and receive strength from the Holy Spirit through prayer and the laying on of hands by a Bishop.

123. *What is required of those to be confirmed?*
    It is required of those to be confirmed that they have been baptized, are sufficiently instructed in the Christian faith, are

penitent for their sins, and are ready to affirm their confession of Jesus Christ as Savior and Lord.

124. *What is Ordination?*
Ordination is the rite in which God gives authority and the grace of the Holy Spirit, through prayer and the laying on of hands by a Bishop, to those being made Bishops, Priests and Deacons.

125. *What is Christian Marriage?*
Christian Marriage, sometimes called holy matrimony, is a lifelong union into which the woman and the man enter when they make their vows before God and the Church and receive the grace of God to help them fulfill their vows.

126. *What is Confession and Absolution?*
Confession and Absolution, sometimes called the Reconciliation of a Penitent, or Penance, is the rite in which those who repent of their sins may confess them to God in the presence of a Priest and receive the assurance of pardon and the grace of Absolution.

127. *What is the Anointing of the Sick?*
The Anointing of the Sick, sometimes called Unction, is the anointing of the sick with oil. By this God's grace is given for the healing of spirit, mind, and body.

128. *Is God's activity limited to these rites?*
God does not limit himself to these rites; they are patterns of countless ways by which God uses material things to reach out to us.

129. *How are the sacraments related to our Christian hope?*
Sacraments sustain our present hope and anticipate its future fulfillment.

Angels

130. *What is an angel?*
An angel is a spiritual creature and part of God's great unseen world.

131. *Why are angels important to us?*
Beyond being messengers of God, angels are guardians to

human beings against danger and temptation, and they watch over children. They remind us that we are part of a great spiritual world that is bound up with our material world.

132. *Is belief in angels scriptural?*
Yes. Mention of angels is found frequently in both the Old and New Testaments. The Bible refers to cherubim, seraphim, archangels, and guardian angels. Angels played a significant role in the life and teaching of Jesus Christ.

133. *Are all angels good?*
All angels were created good by God, but some rebelled against him and became his enemy. They are called demons, and their leader is Satan, the devil.

134. *Do demons have the power to harm Christians?*
The power of God is always stronger than the power of demons. Those who trust in God and call on Jesus as Lord and Savior have the victory.

135. *What is the Church called to do for people who are afflicted or possessed by evil spirits?*
In the power of Jesus the Church can put to flight all forces that enslave people, so that peace and health can be fully established in people places. The individual Christian is called to trust at all times in the protection of the blood of Jesus.

The Christian Hope

136. *What is the Christian hope?*
The Christian hope is to live in newness and fullness of life, and to await the coming of Christ in glory, and the completion of God's purpose for the world.

137. *What do we mean by the coming of Christ in glory?*
By the coming of Christ in glory we mean that Christ will come not in weakness but in power, and he will make all things new.

138. *What do we mean by heaven and hell?*
By heaven we mean eternal life in our enjoyment of God; by hell we mean eternal death in our rejection of God.

139. *Why do we remember the dead in prayer?*
We remember them because we still hold them in our love, and

because we trust that in God's presence those who have chosen to serve him will grow in his love until they see him as he is.

140. *What do we mean by the Last Judgment?*
We believe that Christ will come in glory and judge the living and the dead.

141. *What do we mean by the resurrection of the body?*
We mean that God will raise us from death in the fullness of our being, that we may live with Christ in the communion of saints.

142. *What is the communion of saints?*
The communion of saints is the family of God, the living and the dead, those whom we love and those whom we hurt, bound together in Christ by sacrament, prayer, and praise.

143. *What do we mean by everlasting life?*
By everlasting life we mean a new existence in which we are united with all the people of God, in the joy of fully knowing God and each other.

144. *What, then, is our assurance as Christians?*
Our assurance as Christians is that nothing, not even death, shall separate us from the love of God that is in Christ Jesus our Lord. Amen.

Anglican Spirituality
The Most Reverend Frank T. Griswold
Presiding Bishop and Primate
The Episcopal Church in the United States

We experience around us a yearning for meaning in the face of life's precariousness. The signs are everywhere. This yearning is variously addressed in both healthy and unhealthy ways, more and less effective. Attention to the life of the Spirit is among them. Unfortunately, some of this attention is in the nature of a passing fancy, unmoored from the received tradition or the wisdom of the ages. Our Anglican heritage is a rich treasure for us in these times, to take ever more deeply to ourselves, and to share with a searching world.

Anglican spirituality is a fruit of our profoundly incarnational theology, and it has to do with what the eighteenth-century Priest-mystic, William Law, calls "the process of Christ." Through daily encounters with the risen One in word and sacrament, and in the events and circumstances that challenge and mold us, we are transformed and conformed to the pattern of Christ.

Anglican spirituality places an emphasis on the developmental nature of grace and therefore attends carefully to time. The day, the week, the season, the year, the span of a person's life are all ordered to "the process of Christ." Put differently, Christ happens to us over time. The One who makes use of water, bread, and wine to mediate his presence can make use of the stuff of our lives and relationships to address us and draw us more deeply into his life, death, and resurrection.

For Anglicans, our various prayer books provide for the ordering of time in such a way that we meet Christ in the unfolding of our lives both personally and corporately. Baptism—whether as infants, or as adults after a lengthy catechumen—constitutes our being "born again," our being incorporated in Christ's risen body by sharing symbolically in his dying and in his rising. From that point on, until the moment of our actual death, we are growing in maturity in Christ (Ephesians 4:13). As St. Augustine of Hippo put it, "we become who we are," namely extensions of Christ in time and space by virtue of our being limbs of his body, the Church, of which he is the head. The Eucharist, then, becomes the sign and symbol of our "growing up in Christ." It represents one regular and sustained encounter with Christ in the power of the Spirit.

Because Jesus Christ is the incarnate and glorified word of God, fundamental to all spirituality is the capacity and willingness on the part of persons of faith to listen. "Oh that today you would hearken to his voice!" we are counseled in Psalm 96, which is used throughout the Anglican Communion as an Invitatory at Morning Prayer. As each day begins we are invited to listen to the words and events that lie ahead "as those who are taught" (Isaiah 50:4).

Because Christ is the word of God, it is Christ who addresses us through the word of Holy Scripture. Indeed, the Bible broadly conceived is a sacrament: It is "alive and active, sharper than a two-edged sword" because Christ is alive and active and truly present in the scriptural word. The risen One who opened the Scriptures to his downcast disciples on the road to Emmaus (Luke 24) continues to make our hearts burn within us as the Holy Spirit, the Spirit of truth, draws from what is Christ's (John 16:14) and makes it known to us in the context of our own life and experience. The fact that Jesus had more to say to his disciples than they could presently bear or assimilate (John 16:12) makes it clear that God's word in Christ continues to "go forth" in its ever-creative potentiality, and to reveal new meaning, and to speak to new situations in our lives, personally and as communities of faith, with our distinctive cultures, histories, and challenges.

In the Hebrew, "word" carried with it notions of occurrence as well as speech. Words therefore happen; they take place. The sacraments and sacramental rites are enacted words whose force and power once again derive from the risen One. "You have revealed yourself to me, O Christ, face to face. I have met you in your sacraments." These bold words of St. Ambrose underscore the formative and developmental effect of our sacramental participation in season and out of season, and at the different turnings of our lives. Listening to the word who is Christ also involves listening to our lives, to the events and circumstances, momentous and ordinary. Each and all are shot through with meaning. We are required as well to listen to the continuously unfolding life and experience of our national churches, and the larger Anglican and world communion of which we are a part. Our careful listening to one another moves, then, from an expression of polite interest to a theological enterprise of the first order.

In the Acts of the Apostles we are told how the word of God "spread" and "grew mightily" (13:49; 19:20), and how the apostles' safely circumscribed world of first-century Judaism was turned upside down and inside out by manifestations of Christ and the Holy Spirit in unlikely and highly problematical circumstances, which defied all precedence and reduced the apostolic community to proclaiming, "for it has seemed good to the Holy Spirit and to us" (15:28).

Anglican spirituality also involves a "graced pragmatism," a reasonableness conformed to the mind of Christ, a capacity for "testing the spirits" (1 John 4:1) of our contemporary world and existence in order to hear and be faithful to Christ, the word who can speak and reveal himself in the Scripture of our own lives and experience, as well as in the Bible, the sacraments, and the ongoing life of the Church.

As we live "the process of Christ" and "become who we are," our most ordinary and seemingly random experiences give intimations of the divine. This is the gift of Anglican spirituality—our gift to receive with gratitude, and to share.

When Anglicans Worship
The Reverend Paul Gibson

Anglican worship is based on the principle that God's will for the world has been made known in Jesus Christ, and that we may discover what that means when we worship together in Church and so realize it in the whole of our lives. Anglicans worship because we are people of God's kingdom and because we believe that by God's grace our Church worship may empower our life worship.

The English word "worship" may help us understand this. It is a very old word. Its root meaning is "honour." Today when we speak of worship, we mostly use the word to talk about our relationship with God, but it used to have a wider meaning. In the marriage service in older Anglican prayer books, the groom gives a ring to his bride with the words, "With this ring I thee wed, with my body I thee worship." His vow did not mean he was going to treat her as divine. It meant that he promised to behave towards her in a way that honored her completely. The word "worship" is still used in a similar way in some countries where magistrates and other high civic officials are addressed as "Your worship." We treat them with honour because they represent the authority and dignity of the community.

The Big Picture: Worship as the Way We Live

This old way of using the English word for worship tells us something about its root meaning: Worship is about behavior, about acting toward another with honour. The same principle applies to our worship of God. Worship is about the way we live, about honoring the creator by fulfilling the highest purposes of creation. Worship is the thankful return of creation to its source, which for human beings means living in justice, responsibility, and love. One of the greatest leaders of the early Church wrote: "The glory of God is humanity fully alive." Worship is about being in a state of glorious wholeness.

Compilers of the English Liturgy

A. Bp. Cranmer
Bp. Ridley   Bp. Goodrich
Bp. Holbech   Bp. Skip
Bp. Thirlby   Bp. Day
Dr. Taylor   Dr. Cox
Dr. May Haynes Redmayne Robertson

Anglicans have always been committed to the unbreakable relationship between worship in the Church and worship in daily life.

The "Small Picture": Worship as Formation

There is another, smaller picture, but it is also important. It is defined by our human need to be shaped, formed, and converted into the kind of people who worship with our lives. We learn to praise with our lives by praising with our lips; we learn to live in thankful response to God by giving thanks daily for the blessings of life, for forgiveness and renewal. We learn the pathways of justice by greeting one another as the children of God, by accepting all those with whom we share the experience of the cleansing water, and by sharing the food over which we have proclaimed God's saving love in words of thanksgiving.

We need the "small picture" of worship in order to become people of the big picture of worship. We need worship in the form of liturgy, the kind of activity we do in church, in order to be people of life worship.

The Danger of Liturgy

One of the worst things that can happen in the whole realm of religion is that the small-picture model of worship should become an end to itself. The Bible is very emphatic on this point. Again and again the prophets of the Old Testament accused their people of this terrible misunderstanding.

The prophet Micah wrote:

> "With what shall I come before the LORD, and bow myself before God on high? Shall I come before him with burnt offerings, with calves a year old? Will the LORD be pleased with thousands of rams, with ten thousand rivers of oil? Shall I give my firstborn for my transgression, the fruit of my body for the sin of my soul?" He has told you, O mortal, what is good; and what does the LORD require of you but to do justice, and to love kindness, and to walk humbly with your God? (6:6–8, NRSV)

And the author of the second part of the book of Isaiah, addressing people who could not understand why God had not answered the prayers they had offered with fasting, asked them:

> Is it not the fast that I choose: to loose the bonds of injustice, to undo the thongs of the yoke, to let the oppressed go free, and to break

every yoke? Is it not to share your bread with the hungry, and bring the homeless poor into your house; when you see the naked, to cover them, and not to hide yourself from your own kin? Then your light shall break forth like the dawn, and your healing shall spring up quickly; your vindicator shall go before you, the glory of the LORD, shall be your rear guard. (58:6–8, NRSV)

Jesus stood in the tradition of the prophets when he said the Sabbath was made for people and not people for the Sabbath, when he quoted Isaiah's words condemning those who honored God with their lips but not with their hearts, and when he told the story of the despised outsider who cared for a wonderful man when two religious leaders passed him by, finishing with the question, "Which of these three, do you think, was a neighbor to the man who fell into the hands of the robbers?" (Luke 10:36, NRSV).

Anglican Worship as Life Worship

Anglicans have always given a great deal of attention to worship in the form of liturgy. One of the most significant moments in the process of the English Reformation was the publication of the Book of Common Prayer, with its commitment to worship in the language of the people, to proclamation of the Scriptures in a systematic and comprehensible manner, and to rites that are rooted in tradition but simple enough to be followed easily.

Anglican liturgy developed in a number of directions in the course of time, many of them suggesting a love of beauty and quiet restraint that have come to typify Anglicanism for many people. But other forms of Anglican worship are passionate and enthusiastic. Whatever Anglican worship has looked like, it is worship (and we believe we do), what God wants ultimately is the life worship of justice, responsibility, and love.

The Christian Sacrifice

Our Anglican commitment to life worship is woven into the fabric of our tradition of Church worship. When Anglicans join together in a general confession of sin, we pray (in the words of the Book of Common Prayer) that our hearts may be set to obey God's commandments and that we may walk in holiness and righteousness all

The Church proclaims the whole faith to all people. In the Sudan.

our days. When we ask that we may walk in holiness and right-eousness all our days, we are praying about a conversion of our personal and social style of living, and not only about an inner cleansing. In the prayers that surround the sharing of bread and wine at the Lord's table we offer and present to God "ourselves, our souls and bodies, to be a reasonable, holy, and living sacrifice." In these prayers we are talking about the way we treat not only our families, friends, and neighbors, but the way we behave toward people who are rejected and despised (the people Jesus befriended), and the way we organize our towns and cities and respect our lands, forests, and water.

The liturgy's reference to our souls and bodies as "sacrifice" is important. Of course Anglicans believe that Jesus' self-giving is the "full, perfect, and sufficient sacrifice" that can never be repeated. But we, as his followers, are taken into his sacrifice and its transforming power by giving thanks in the worship we do together when we gather as a Christian community, and by living in a style in which (to use Paul's words) we "present our bodies as a living sacrifice, holy and acceptable to God, which is our spiritual worship" (Romans 12:1). The author of the letter to the Ephesians said the same thing when he told his readers to, "live in love, as Christ loved us and gave himself up for us, a fragrant offering and sacrifice to God" (Eph. 5:2). Our sacrifice is living to God's glory, as that living is described in thanksgiving and rooted in the crucial self-giving of Jesus, our Lord.

Liturgy and Life

Frederick Denison Maurice, one of the great Anglican theologians of the nineteenth-century, warned Anglicans against treating their forms of Church worship as an end in themselves. He said he hoped no one would ever hear him talk about "our excellent and incomparable liturgy." He said we should not praise our liturgy, but use it for our life. "When we do not want it for our life," he wrote, "we may begin to talk of it as a beautiful composition: Thanks be to God it does not remind us of its own merits when it is bidding us to draw nigh to him."

The first Anglican prayer books were rooted in the ancient worship tradition of the church. In the course of time they were modified to reflect particular theological and regional expressions. More recently they have been supplemented and sometimes replaced by contemporary texts. But the whole tradition has always been committed to the unbreakable relationship of Church worship and life worship. This is why some of our modern liturgies end with the doxology.

> Glory to God, whose power working in us, can do far more than we can ask or imagine. Glory to God, from generation to generation, in the Church and in Jesus Christ, now and for ever. Amen.

Mission
The Anglican Consultative Council, 1990

There has been a consistent view of mission repeated by the Anglican Consultative Council (ACC), the Lambeth Conference, the Primates Meeting, and others in recent years. It defines mission in a fourfold way:

The mission of the Church is as follows:

(a) to proclaim the good news of the kingdom;

(b) to teach, baptize, and nurture new believers;

(c) to respond to human need by loving service;

(d) to seek to transform the unjust structures of society.

We now feel that our understanding of the ecological crisis, and indeed the threats to the unity of all creation, mean that we have to add a fifth affirmation:

(e) to strive to safeguard the integrity of creation and sustain and renew the life of the earth.

Two important elements of this definition have tended to be particularly stressed within the Inter-Anglican structures: (1) The call to the Decade of Evangelism has stressed proclamation of the Gospel, but usually this is clearly defined in a way that is related to the other elements of the definition; and (2) The idea of transformation has also been developing and needs to be more widely recognized. ACC-6 used a definition of transformation borrowed from the International Evangelical Consultation on the Nature and Mission of the Church (1983): "a change from a level human existence that is less than that envisaged by our wholeness in harmony with

The mission of the Church is to restore all people to unity with God and with each other in Christ. The Secretary General in a Brazilian Favela.

God, with fellow human beings, and with every aspect of his environment." The Lambeth Conference 1988 issued a pastoral letter entitled "On the Gospel and Transformation," which said, "Some lay stress on inner personal change, others on social and political change. But increasingly, as we have learned from each other and grown in commitment to each other, we realize the real task into which Jesus Christ is sending us all. We must hold these varied emphases together in one Gospel and one witness in the one body."

The concept of transformation can be a corrective to any tendency to isolate evangelism from social responsibility. The Decade of Evangelism must also be a decade of transformation.

History and Vision

Anglicans have a great sense of history and a desire to honor tradition. In Wales.

The Suffering Church

An address by The Reverend Canon John L. Peterson,
Secretary General, to the National Assembly of the
Anglican Church of Australia, 1997

The Church of the Lord is built upon the rock of the apostles, yet among so many dangers in the world it remains unmoved. The Church's foundation is firm and unshakeable against assaults of the raging sea. Waves lash at the Church but do not shatter it. Although the elements of this world constantly beat upon the Church with crashing sounds, the Church possesses the safest harbour of salvation for all in distress.

There is a stream which flows down on God's saints like a torrent. There is a rushing river giving joy to the heart. It is at peace and makes for peace.

It is with the assurance of these quotations from the letters of St. Ambrose that I approach prayerfully the topic set before me at this great gathering of Anglicans in Australia—the suffering Church. Indeed, we as a global family have within our membership the reality of that suffering, persecution, injustice, and oppression. All of these elements are alive and well in the Church today, tormenting and tearing at the lives of faithful Anglican Christians like you and me, day by day and hour by hour.

A prayer in last year's Anglican Cycle of Prayer puts it well:

O Saviour Christ, in whose way of love lies the secret of all life and the hope of all people, we pray for the quiet courage to match this hour. We did not choose to be born or to live in such an age; but let its problems challenge us, its discoveries exhilarate us, its injustices anger us, its possibilities inspire us, and its vigour renew us, for your kingdom's sake.

Rwanda. The horrors of the situation of the Church in Rwanda is foremost in many of our thoughts and prayers. The Church there is in terrible turmoil. It experienced suffering and in some cases gave

Anglicans seek to be the hands, arms, and eyes of Jesus Christ in the world today. The Primate of the Indian Ocean on the Via Dolorosa.

in to that suffering, failing itself and the Lord. The structures of the Church have been shattered, the leadership is scattered, the situation is intolerable. The faithful cry for help, leaders are rare and hard to find. Those who are living out the trials and tribulations of either returning to Rwanda or, after having been in exile, simply trying to maintain their status in society, face persecution, harassment, and sometimes even the threat of death. Our Anglican brothers and sisters in Rwanda are hurting. The threat of persecution is still very much there. The situation is desperate. We as a Communion need to act, and yet we in some ways have our hands tied. From my visits to Rwanda let me share with you a few of the most incredible sights I have ever seen in my life.

Who could ever forget walking through a Church where the skeletons of five thousand people are still lying on the floor?

Who could ever forget walking through the same Church and seeing blood-stained clergy stoles strewn on the floor amongst the bones of the victims of the genocide?

Who could ever forget visiting an Anglican orphanage and seeing hundreds of orphans, who will carry the horror of the genocide with them every day of their life?

Who could ever forget walking into a Church and the crowd of one thousand who greeted me, who were all widows? All of their husbands had been murdered, including the Dean of the Anglican Cathedral in Kigali.

But the image from Rwanda that will always haunt me is neither Hutu nor Tutsi; instead, it is of an impoverished Pigmy community living alongside a Rwandan hill. I was with Alison from Christian Aid when we stopped to see this community. Its people had fled at the time of the genocide, and their impoverished homes were looted and ransacked. When they returned home everything was gone, including the makeshift walls of their homes. They had nothing left. No housing. No food. Nothing. A mother, perhaps fifteen years old, was feeding her child. All of a sudden the child slapped his mother's breast and grabbed the other breast. Then the child started to scream. There was no milk in his mother's breasts. When Alison asked the mother what she needed, her only request was for some milk for her child. The mother did not ask for a car. The mother did not ask for a bicycle. The mother did not ask for a television or a VCR. The mother wanted only some milk for her child. The mother had no food, she was malnourished, her breasts had gone dry. And every Pigmy mother whom we saw was dry. We are Rwanda when our voice of outrage does not join that child's scream. How can we enable the local Church to speak to such distress?

Sudan. What can one say about the Sudan? Here is a Church that lives and moves and has its being in the grasp of the most horrific persecution of any body of Christians today. Our brother and sister Anglicans in the Episcopal Church in the Sudan, which numbers hundreds of thousands, especially in the south of the Sudan, face the constant threat of civil war, malnourishment, and abject poverty, not knowing where a piece of cloth for clothing or some rice or meal for food may come from next. Our brother and sister Anglicans face this reality day by day, moment by moment.

Our fellow Anglicans around the world experience the reality of not having water for baptism, or bread and wine for communion. These things, which many take for granted, are a real luxury in their lives.

What is their response? Their response is what the Archbishop of Canterbury described as some of the most stirring and uplifting testimonies of faith, love, and Christian community that he has ever seen in his ministry. The Church of Jesus Christ amongst our Episcopalian friends is growing and vibrant and alive. Alive because it believes and practises what it preaches.

Northern Ireland. We are blessed with excellent leadership in the Church of Ireland, the Church of the Anglican Communion in that troubled land. Suffering is constant; the suffering is great. It penetrates many levels of society, from young to old. Here a first-world, prosperous country lives in the pangs of hatred, bigotry, death, and destruction day by day, hour by hour. And yet the Church of Jesus Christ takes its stand against the wrongs that are perpetrated on all sides—takes its stand to be alongside the suffering, the mournful, to be the valiant Church of Jesus Christ. We can be proud of our Anglican brothers and sisters and their witness to the radical Gospel of Christ's love in the midst of all this clamour, confusion, and pain.

There is more suffering. Indeed there is, whether it be in Dunblane, Scotland, or Port Arthur, or the tiny congregation of faithful Anglicans who come together early in the evening of Christmas Eve for their Christmas Eucharist. Their hearts' desire is to celebrate the nativity of our Lord at midnight, as Christians do all over the world, but the street crime and the violence in their sophisticated, developed neighbourhood are too much to handle; the risk is too high. This too is suffering, as people in this congregation become prisoners in their own backyards.

Palestine. Another form of suffering being experienced by Anglicans is living under occupation, having lost everything—homes and land having been confiscated. Today in Jerusalem, the City of the Resurrection, our brothers and sisters in Jesus Christ suffer. Last Christmas Eve, Anglicans were prevented from going to their Cathedral to worship, not because of street crime or violence, but because basic human rights were denied them.

I always remember an experience I had with Patti Browning, the wife of the Presiding Bishop of the Episcopal Church in the United States. One afternoon we went to our hospital in Nablus. Nablus is in the centre of the West Bank. Ever since 1987, when the Intifada began, the people of Nablus had suffered tremendously. Their city had frequently been under curfew for days at a time (no one was allowed outside of their homes; it was like house arrest). Many homes had been broken into and searched by the soldiers. Many young men had been dragged off to detention centres or prisons, not to be heard from for weeks at a time. Many people had been beaten, had limbs broken. While we were at St. Luke's Hospital in Nablus, a hospital owned by our Church, Patti spoke to many of the patients. As she spoke to them, she could hear the shootings and the demonstrations outside the hospital walls. One Palestinian woman had just, within the hour, given birth. As she held her baby for Patti to see, Patti asked the baby's name. She was told, through the translator, that the child would be called "Salaam"—"Peace."

What a moving, eloquent prayer. In the midst of shootings and demonstrations outside her hospital window, a mother named her child "Peace." That mother was certainly realistic about the setting into which her child was born, but then in the midst of shootings, demonstrations, and death, she named her child "Peace." That mother knew that her child's life would not be free of struggle, but more importantly she prayed that her child's life would be marked by and filled with an ever-present love. That would be the peace of which she would be the living reminder. That Palestinian woman in Nablus had given her answer—Peace, Salaam. Peace now was her prayer, knowing that her affirmation would not make the demonstrations or the retaliations stop, but also knowing that every moment presents us with an opportunity to state and to live our commitment to the peace of God for which we pray, and for which we must work.

Suffering is experienced on many levels. Certainly it is in the dramatic stories that we hear from the Sudans and Rwandans of this world. But suffering also exists in the hearts, minds, and lives of people marginalised by society, even by the Church. Suffering takes many forms. Depression, divorce, disquietude, disenchantment; all speak clearly of the level of human suffering in our world today. Suffering knows no barriers of race, colour, gender, or age, but guess what—neither does redemption. Neither does our own transformation know any of these barriers.

To understand suffering is to be at one with the Psalmist:

> The LORD is close to the brokenhearted and saves those who are crushed in spirit. O LORD, you have searched me and known me. You know when I sit down and when I rise, you perceive my thoughts from afar, you discern my going out and my lying down. You are familiar with all my ways. (34:18, 139:1–3)

As Christians, how can we ever forget the promise in 1 Peter: "Cast all your anxiety on him, because he cares for you" (5:7). As Anglicans, we cherish our heritage in the living word of God and in the living Son of God, our Lord Jesus Christ. We are guaranteed beyond all shadow of doubt that God, when he created this world, created something that was very good. Yet as we all know, sin, death, and destruction entered the world through one person. But that is not the end of the story, because the people of the Sudan, Northern Ireland, Palestine, and the small Australian neighbourhood Church I described all praise and honour and worship the living God, revealed in Jesus Christ. We all know the familiar passage: "God so loved the world that he gave his only Son, that whoever believes in him shall not perish but have everlasting life. For God did not send his Son into the world to condemn the world, but to save the world through him" (John 3:16–17). Jesus cares. The entire ministry of Jesus Christ was a ministry of caring. He went about the towns and villages, teaching in the synagogues and preaching good news and healing every disease and sickness. As St. Matthew tells us, "When he saw the crowds he had compassion on them" (Matt. 14:4).

And what is the response of the world to the caring, loving Saviour? We all know what that is. And as we approach Lent, we know that Jesus suffered death, shared in our humanity, and through his death might destroy its power and free us whose lives are held in slavery by the fear of death.

Our brothers and sisters in some of the most tormented, devastated parts of the world believe that wholeheartedly. The trauma they face in their daily lives is overcome by faith in the living Christ. What does that teach you and me, those of us who in our religiosity spend hours of energy and anxiety over all the minutiae that comes across our desks as concerns of the Church. Where are our priorities as we face the new millennium? Where are our priorities as we look for a new heaven and a new earth?

I have a friend who told me that about twenty years ago he went through a bout of major depression. He didn't know what was coming, he wasn't sure what caused it at the time. But suddenly his life was shattered by depression. Through that depression, however, this friend found release and freedom—liberation and salvation. Because of the depression, the suffering forced him to come to grips with who he was, what life was about, and who God was in his life—a God whom he worshipped and studied and was aware of on some level for many, many years, but never really encountered until this moment of truth. Ours is not a pie-in-the-sky faith. We are a real living global family. I pray to God that we will be more appreciative of that fact, realising that we can learn from each other on all levels; the suffering people of Rwanda teach us a lesson, the suffering people of Sudan can teach us a lesson. The frightened people of suburbia teach us a lesson. The frightened people of Northern Ireland or the Middle East can teach us a lesson. What are those lessons? Faithfulness, sharing, empowerment, love, concern, prayer, and so much more.

What is our obligation in all this? What is the message to us in the Anglican Communion? Of course, among one of the greatest ministries we have with each other is that of prayer. I think of the images in the fifth chapter of the Epistle of James, speaking of the anointing of the sick, and how the Scripture tells us that the prayer offered in faith by the Church will make the sick person well. The Lord will raise him up, and yet Paul reminds us that even in our weakness there is strength: "My grace is sufficient for you, because my power is made perfect in weakness" (2 Corinthians 12:9). We are hard pressed on every side, but not crushed; perplexed, but not in despair; persecuted, but not abandoned. Indeed, our Church, the Anglican Communion, must be powerful in the witness and testimony of the truth of these illustrations from Scripture. But the needs are monumental and on many levels. We must strengthen our commitment of faith, not wallow in isolation. We must work together as a global family, so graciously given to us by God; we must be open to the Spirit of renewal and strength as we seek to be the hands, the arms, and the eyes of Jesus Christ in this world today.

In Jerusalem I particularly like the Church at the First Station of the Cross. Here, in the Church that remembers Jesus being condemned, is a mosaic of the crown of thorns, which adorns the sanctuary dome. A crown of thorns. A crown of thorns worn by a King. Kings and queens in our world do not wear crowns of thorns. They wear crowns of gold, silver, and other precious metals, set with diamonds, emeralds, rubies, and other precious stones. That is what royalty wears. But the King of Kings and Lord of Lords, our King, wears a crown of thorns, a crown that pierces the skin, a crown that causes blood to flow. At the First Station of the Cross we are confronted head-on with a divine reversal. God turns everything we hold so precious absolutely upside down. All the things that we hold so dear—wealth, power, security—are replaced by a crown of thorns. Everything that seems to give us meaning in life—authority, prestige, our own self-importance—is turned upside down by a crown of thorns. At the First Station of the Cross we see God turning society upside down as his Son wears a crown of thorns.

In Dr. Bruce Kaye's book, I have read some of the realities of the work and witness of Anglicans working throughout Australia. I thank God for what he has done and for what he is doing. Dr. Kaye says

> The Anglican Church has indeed a long and honourable record in serving others in society. The vast and extensive welfare services of the Church are ample testimony to that. The pastoral care which is exercised in a thousand different ways in the parishes of our Church is further, though less public, testimony. Of course, that service has not been perfect and is not perfect. We do not and cannot claim to be perfect. The General Confession rightly stands prominently in our liturgy and our gatherings. There are things which we have left undone which we ought to have done, and there are things which we have done which we ought not to have done. Nonetheless, the commitment of our Church in serving this society is a commitment of which we can be justly proud and thankful.

Yet I still offer you a challenge. What will you do in the future? What difference can you make in the lives of your fellow Anglicans around the world, who need you, who need your friendship and support in so many ways? And how can they help you and share with you through their lives? How can they share with you the reality of the vibrant faith they have? I believe that, as he has done before, God puts in front of us opportunity after opportunity, and as we approach the year 2000, may it be a unique time for us and for the Anglican Communion to hold its head high, to be grateful for its heritage, and to commit itself to a liveliness of spirit, sharing, and commitment.

Indeed, when the people of the Sudan suffer, the people in Sydney suffer.

Indeed, when the people of Rwanda suffer, the people in Perth suffer.

Indeed, when the people of Palestine suffer, the people in Melbourne suffer.

Indeed, when the people of Port Arthur suffer, the people in Darwin suffer.

Indeed, when the people of Northern Ireland suffer, the people in Canberra suffer.

I would like to conclude with another story from Sudan. It seems to me that Sudan provides a challenge for all of us, as we look forward to the challenge we have at Christmas and in the new millennium.

Last year I received a letter from Bishop Daniel in the Sudan. The letter was nine pages long, written out in longhand. To be absolutely honest, it sat on my desk a couple of days before I read it because it was so long and because it was handwritten. At the start of the letter the Bishop was telling me about the horrid drought in the Sudan and how the drought was ravaging his country. As I continued to read his letter, I gasped upon reading the eighth page. The Bishop wrote about his son John who had died in February. He died in a refugee camp of either malaria or some other unknown disease. The Bishop did not know why his son died. The Bishop asked that we pray for his son, for John's wife, and for his two small daughters. Then he asked for our prayers for Mama Grace, his wife. John's death had been terrible for her. The Bishop asked for no money. He asked only for prayers for his people and for his family. Ravaged. Devastated. The people of the Sudan, like the Rwandans, Burundians, Kurds, and Palestinians, all know what it means to suffer. Members of our family are suffering.

Let us pray:

> Dear Lord, you are the truth. When I keep myself rooted in you I will live in the truth. Help me, Lord, to live a truthful life, a life where I am guided not by popularity, public opinion, current fashion, or convenient formulations, but by a knowledge that comes from knowing you. There may be times during which holding on to the truth is hard and painful, and leads to oppression, persecution, and even death. Be with me, Lord, if that time ever comes. Let me then experience that to hold on to the truth means to hold on to you, that love and truth can never be separated, and that to live truthfully is the same as being faithful to a loving relationship. We must all work on this together; there can be no missing links. Jesus, may all that is you flow into me. May your body and blood be my food and drink. May your passion and death be my strength and life. Jesus, with you by my side, enough has been given. May the shelter I seek be the shadow of your cross. Let me not run from the love that you offer, but hold me safe from the forces of evil. On each of my dyings shed your light and your love. Keep calling to me until that day comes when, with your saints, I may praise you forever.

God bless you all.

Shalom: Living with Differences—The Contribution of the Anglican Communion

A lecture by the Archbishop of Canterbury George Leonard Carey at Northwestern University, May 22, 1996

It was a bomb that both destroyed his life and made it. There was nothing exceptional about the middle-aged Irish man who approached the Market Square in Enniskillen in Northern Ireland to take part in the 1985 Remembrance Day service. Gordon Wilson was a contented Christian man who was as concerned as anyone about the conflicts going on in Northern Ireland, but he saw little point in getting too involved. His only daughter, a nurse, was off duty that day, and they were standing side by side when the bomb went off. He was badly wounded, and she was killed. Her last words were: "Daddy, I love you so much."

Those six words were to be the spur to a crusade for peace that ended only when Gordon died in front of his typewriter a few months ago. His wife, who found him dead, said that there was an extraordinary stillness in the room. Gordon seemed so still, so peaceful. He had just finished the part of his memoirs that told the story of his beloved daughter. Now God had called him to be with her.

The extraordinary thing about Gordon's crusade was his remarkable ability to forgive. The tears of anguish were there, of course, but there was no bitterness, no anger—just love and a fierce unremitting commitment to make an abiding contribution to a peace that would lead to no more broken bodies, scarred minds, and divided communities.

Shalom. The Hebrew word is well known and so is its Arab derivative *Salaam. Salaam alykum* will greet any visitor who visits a Muslim home in the Middle East. But shalom means much more than "hello." It is one of the richest words in the Bible. It is used in many different contexts and refers to so many different things. In many ways it is a portmanteau word that tempts one to import into it more than it can really bear. I must resist that temptation, but we can say with confidence that it means "that quality of life that is expressed in personal spirituality, social and material life, and supremely in the Person of Jesus Christ, the Prince of Peace."

A famous passage in the Old Testament describes a dream we all share—that of all nations surrendering weapons of war for instruments of peace, swords becoming plowshares and spears becoming pruning hooks. "And they shall not learn war anymore," (Is. 2:4) the passage wistfully ends.

Micah adds to Isaiah's version that every man would sit under his vine and fig tree. It is the ideal picture of a small landowner content with life and living in harmony with all people. Sadly, how different was the reality then—and is now. We live in a deeply divided world in which war is more of a reality than peace. We are told that at any given time more than one hundred wars and violent disputes are raging. Sadly there is a ring of truth about the story of the Mid West Newspaper during a period one August when there was hardly anything to report. A boy reporter rushed into the editor's office. "Chief," he said, "what are we going to write? There are no rapes, no murders, and no mass prison break-outs!" To which the editor said calmly, "Relax, young man. I have faith in human nature!"

Individually, nationally, internationally, and across the different faith communities, we acknowledge that shalom is a quality lacking in our world, one that we desperately need to acquire.

At the outset it is important to recognise the fact that religion is often as much a part of the problem as it is a part of the answer. As we look at the world today, religion must own up to its responsibility in dividing communities and inciting bloodshed. While no responsible religious leader would, of course, condone evil, murder, violence, and injustice there is blood on our hands through creating, however innocently, the conditions that create intolerance and fear. Only once we recognise that can the process of building God's shalom in a world of differences begin.

But what contribution can the Anglican Communion make to the search for God's shalom? Indeed, why single out the Anglican Communion at all? After all we are just a tiny Communion of about 70+ million adherents. Small as we are, though, I believe there are several features in our history, theology, and development that are worth noting and sharing with other faith communities, as a contribution to our common calling to be peacemakers.

First we can share our history. Years ago when I was a young curate in a London Church and leading several boys' clubs, one boy sent me an unusual birthday card. It showed a man looking into a mirror. The caption read: "You are not entirely useless. You can always serve as a bad example!" We all have skeletons in our cupboards, and this is certainly true of the history of religions. Anglicanism grew out of the bitter conflicts of the Reformation period. The Church of England became a national Church like so many others on mainland Europe. As Church and nation were seen as one another, religious expressions were banned. Roman Catholicism was suppressed because it was seen as the religion of foreign powers.

But other Christian expressions of faith were suppressed too— the Puritans, Anabaptists, and all those whose forms of worship lay outside the Prayer Book. Later when the Puritans came to power, the Church of England was on the receiving end. Anglican worship was silenced for a few years and all Anglican clergy were deprived. So yes, we can serve as a bad example.

Yet, there were also prophets, people who pointed to the depths of faith in order to denounce intolerance. John Locke, one of the most famous philosophers and thinkers of the seventeenth century, who was pleased to call himself a Church of England man, wrote to a critic: "Since you are pleased to enquire what are my thoughts about the mutual Toleration of Christians in their different professions of religion, I must needs answer you freely, that I esteem toleration to be the chief characteristical mark of the True Church."

And alongside the conflicts were such formative examples of reconciliation as the way in which Queen Elizabeth and her advisors dealt with the question of the Eucharist. The issue of transubstantiation, you will recall, was one for which Protestants and Catholics killed and burned each other for years. Deep divisions remained about what exactly happened to the bread and wine. Elizabeth's solution, in a nutshell, was to find a form of words and an attitude that enabled people with different views on this question to remain in the same Church and join together in worship for the sake of all they have in common. Specific doctrinal divisions were held to be less important than the common core of belief and were to be contained rather than allowed to foment schism. This is at the heart of the Anglican tradition.

Second, we can share our theology. Through that painful period of our history that featured the first attempts by Puritans and others to seek freedom and tolerance in the New World, the Church of England was seeking to discover something that was already there in our liturgy and articles: namely, the striving after inclusivism. Whatever the Reformation represents today, in the days of the first English Reformers, the Church as "Catholic" was not questioned. Cranmer, Jewel, Hooker, and others simply did not see themselves as revolutionaries—they were reformers. They were not founding a new Church; it was the same Church as before but now renewed through a return to what was essentially "catholic," rather than to medieval teaching and rites. Cranmer put it so well in his introduction to the Prayer Book: "And, whereas in our time the minds of men are so diverse that some think it a matter of conscience to depart from a piece of the least of their ceremonies . . . . And on the other side some be so new fangled that they would innovate all

"And they shall beat their swords into plowshares . . . neither shall they learn war any more" (Is. 2:4). Site of the martyrdom of St. Thomas à Becket, Canterbury Cathedral.

things and so despise the old . . . it was thought expedient, not so much to have respect how to please and satisfy either of these parties, as how to please God, and profit them both."

What Cranmer fought for in worship was sought in matters of doctrine and life. As we have seen the Anglican tradition has often sought compromise, not just because of old-fashioned English pragmatism, but because we have perceived that there is something deeply Christian about comprehensiveness. We do not believe that any Church possesses the entire Christian truth or that any single tradition can claim to be the sole repository of divine revelation.

Thus, within our body we have sought to hold the diverse strands of Church life, whether it has been evangelical, catholic, liberal or charismatic. We have noted that honourable people have inhabited these traditions and that truth is to be found in them all—but we have not accepted that any one of them has the right to arrogate to itself complete authority, thus de-churching the rest.

Our recent decision to ordain women to the priesthood is an example of the comprehensiveness we have struggled to express. By an overwhelming vote, General Synod decided to accept women for the ordained ministry. This conclusion to twenty years' hard thought and work saddened a significant minority. We could have decided as a Church to ignore them—after all, Synod had made the decision with acclaim. We did not ignore them. We provided alternative pastoral care and made reasonable financial provision available to those who in conscience could not stay in the Church. We were criticised for this generosity. Our talk of "two integrities" was called "theological nonsense." Our pastoral arrangements through three so-called "flying bishops" were criticised as undermining the unity of the Church. Our financial arrangements were criticised as being unnecessary. But a mere two years later the apparent "messiness" of these arrangements has brought a calmness to the Church that has allowed the two integrities on this particular issue to live together in peace for the sake of all we have in common.

This kind of Anglican comprehensiveness carries implicitly, within its being, structured dissent. We are a Communion that has internalised disagreement and lives with it gladly, most of the time. If you like, we are content to live with blurred edges and with some degree of provisionality. This is not to be confused with vagueness, or woolly-mindedness or lack of theological integrity. I have heard it said that the genius of Anglicanism is "that it doesn't matter what you believe as long as you don't take it too seriously." That is nonsense, in the sense that we hold passionately to the core of the faith and are deeply committed to God and his world and to every neighbour. But there is such a thing as Anglican thought, polity, and lifestyle. We are committed to discovering God's truth and making it known. But we are equally ready to live with questions and to resist easy answers.

Third, we can share an experience. I have said that we are a small Communion. However, we are also an international Communion that, now residing in more than 150 countries, lost its Englishness years ago. The Lambeth Conference, which brings bishops from our thirty-six Provinces every ten years, now has an attendance of more than 800. We work among the very poor of the world and we suffer with them. Our Church has its share of martyrs, and we number among our body those who have distinguished themselves in human rights and social justice. I think of Desmond Tutu whose distinguished ministry in South Africa was rewarded with the Nobel Prize. But I think too of South Africa's neighbour, Mozambique, and of Bishop Dinis Singulane, whose contribution toward peace was heroic, self sacrificial, and noteworthy.

Again, in my own country, it is not just people like Gordon Wilson who have striven so hard to bring peace to Northern Ireland. Church leaders have been important mediators for many years. They have been significant partners in the peace process, and none more so than the two Anglican Archbishops, Robin Eames and Donald Caird, along with their Roman Catholic counterpart, Cardinal Daly. Their contributions, as I discovered on my visit there eighteen months ago, are deeply respected and valued by politicians of many shades of opinion, on both sides of the border.

But, alongside these, there are many other stories to tell of the Anglican experience of peace-making. Central to this experience is our theology and its emphasis, the Incarnation of our Lord. Christianity has to be lived out where people suffer and die. It stresses that faith without works lacks true substance and works without faith is but social action. As a result, we have traditionally had a substantial stake in education in many countries around the world—and the multitudes of schools and colleges can be seedbeds of peace-loving values.

Furthermore, we believe in bringing home to people God's protest against anything that dehumanises his world and harms those made in his image and likeness. Anglicanism can be modestly proud of its enormous investment in hospitals, clinics, schools, and homes among the world's poor. My visit to Rwanda last year made me aware of the rich contribution that our Church has made to that country over the years and of how desperately Rwanda needs it now in the task of rebuilding that is going on. Moreover, many Anglican Churches have quite strong national structures as well as a wider international dimension as Provinces within a worldwide communion. This can be a relevant combination in exercising influence in resolving conflicts. For a variety of historical reasons, Anglicans tend to be disproportionately represented among influential elites in many countries, bringing special responsibilities and opportunities. And, within the world of religion, we find ourselves, from our very nature, as a bridge between Protestant and Catholic traditions. Where Roman Catholic and Orthodox churches may at times experience some friction or political tension, Anglicans can sometimes act as interpreters and bridge builders. And these habits of bridge building can then be applied in other dimensions of life.

Therefore, putting the story, the theology, and the experience together, what is the message that comes from within the heart of Anglicanism as we feel the longing in the human family for peace? Let me suggest four principles.

1. *Making room for others.* Article 18 of the Universal Declaration of Human Rights, 1948, declares: "Everyone has the right to freedom of thought, conscience, and religion. This includes the freedom to change his religion or belief . . ." I have called this in several addresses the commitment to "reciprocity." And we must not be half-hearted about it. Muslims, Hindus, Sikhs, and others have equal rights to worship freely in the West and to make disciples just as Christians do. However, this must apply equally to the rights that Christians should have in places where they are in a minority.

2. *Making tolerance central to our beliefs.* Tolerance appears to be in short supply these days. But believers who deny it to others are denying something central to their religious tradition. In all mainstream faiths, tolerance and acceptance of differences are written into our codes. Sadly, the injunctions to respect, honour, and tolerate those of other faiths are not always heeded. And yet terrible things continue to be done in the name of religion, which shames religion and makes it a disgrace.

Therefore we need to ask: Is it not time to espouse a genuine toleration that goes beyond mere acceptance of one another?

True tolerance has something to do with intensity of commitment toward another. Indifference is often confused with tolerance. Baroness Wootton once observed sarcastically, "People are only tolerant about things they don't really care about." But genuine tolerance goes beyond indifference; it travels further than mere co-existence. It ends in risky identification with those whose faiths and lifestyles are different and with a commitment to living and working with them. We need to point to good examples that may provide encouragement and hope in a world damaged by indifference and intolerance alike.

3. *Making room for common action and protest.* If religions are not dying out and may be on the increase in many parts of our world, then religious leadership has a responsibility to resist anything that is done in the name of religion that denies the true ends of religion. I think of extremism that ends in murder and violence. Sometimes when acts perpetrated by fundamentalists occur, I am saddened by the fact that few leaders in such faith communities condemn the atrocities. There can be no justification for acts that leave innocent people dead and wounded. People should not hide behind religious faith to justify acts of terrorism. Prof. Jean

Contemporary expressions of music and liturgy enhance our Christian life.

Kirkpatrick quotes a deeply religious Muslim who remarked: "Please do not call them Muslim fundamentalists. They do not represent a more fundamental version of Islam. They are simply Muslims who are also violent political extremists." Such extremists, wherever they are found—in Egypt, Israel, Northern Ireland or elsewhere—must not find a refuge in religious faith. We must make it clear that true religion does not justify such behaviour. Such extremism must be condemned.

And it is best when we can join in common action against racism, violence, and intolerance together. We must learn to listen to minorities in our communities and seek to give them a voice in raising their concerns. Again, Anglicans have an experience to share here because in so many parts of the world we know what it is like to be a minority. Indeed, small can be beautiful and may be an effective tool for the love of God, especially where that small Church may hold the ring between greater forces than itself. I think of the witness of the Anglican Church in mainland Europe where its congregations, though numerous, can never be seen as serious threats to larger religious communities. As such they are often seen as communities of trust and sometimes as arbiters where disputes scar dialogue.

4. *Holding the tension between the particular and the universal.* We need never be apologetic about the universal claims and integrity of Christian faith. Dialogue and friendship with other faiths do not mean that we sell our soul to the lowest common denominator of faith or to mushy religious-sounding vagueness. I do not believe that all religions are the same and I certainly do not believe that Jesus Christ is merely one great religious figure among others.

Nevertheless, missionary faiths like Christianity and Islam have a duty to look carefully at the tension between making disciples, on the one hand, and respect for other faiths on the other. I believe the task can be done on the basis that faith claims are essentially invitations—invitations to consider that what our experience has meant to us may be something that may transform someone else. That implies that I, too, am obliged to listen to someone else's journey of faith and study the challenge that it brings to me.

In spite of the unique claims of faith communities that must be respected as aspects of religious integrity, we must also note the impressive common ground we all share. Perhaps even here, the Anglican experience of inclusivism and tolerating different points of view has something to offer. On the eve of a new millennium we desperately need to concentrate on what unites us. We owe it to our children and their children to build a more just and peaceful world, a world of tolerance in which love and harmony may flower. This means we need to go deeper into the traditions of our faith and be prepared to study other faiths more positively than we have previously done. As we do so, we shall note that all the great human values that mean so much to us—belief in a purpose beyond ourselves, tolerance, justice, human dignity, love of others, and respect for the elderly, the young, and the vulnerable—are in fact universal religious values. The sacred texts of all religions represent the striving of the human heart for peace. They argue for solidarity and harmony among all people. "Love thy neighbour as thyself" is central to Jesus's summary of the Law. The same sentiment is to be found in all faiths.

There is one final thing that may be shared by us all. It is to join in common witness to the spiritual longings in all human beings. The highest desires of true civilisation are to be found in religious hope and expression. If, as someone once said, the "supreme expression of culture is behaviour," then the sublime ethics of religion at their very best pose an important challenge to anything that diminishes the human spirit. We know that in so many affluent countries a deep moral uncertainty inhibits the embrace of strong moral principles as a guide for generations to come. Young people are growing up with deep spiritual longings that need to be directed into unselfish ends, but they are given little direction. "I shop, therefore I am," has replaced Descartes' "I think, therefore I am." Spiritual communities have resources to challenge the consumerism that lies at the heart of materialistic societies.

We can make an effective contribution to that task only if we put our houses in order. I do not claim that the Communion I represent has all the answers. I can only promise that we intend to go on making our own contribution from within our history, experience, and thought, in common witness with other Christian denominations, and in dialogue with people of other faiths and none.

The decision to ordain women to the priesthood is an example of the comprehensiveness Anglicans have long struggled to express. At Bangor Cathedral.

A friend of mine in England, a black Christian, is concerned about those black communities in Britain that have so much to offer but are hardly given a voice. He told me recently about a little black boy in Britain who was totally withdrawn. He never spoke to anyone at school. Everyone became very worried and a counselor was called in. She said tenderly to him, "Do your parents talk to you?" "No." "Do your brothers and sisters talk to you?" "No." "Do your friends talk to you?" "No." "Does your best friend Mervyn talk to you?" "Oh, yes," came the reply. "And what does he say to you?" asked the counselor. "He tells me to shut up."

Like that little boy, religious communities need to be listened to. Along with our fellow believers, we in the Anglican Communion have much to offer. Yes, there is much bad religion around. The public rhetoric of religion is often bereft of the gentleness and grace that is there in true spirituality. We must all pledge our determination to make a creative contribution to the world as the new millennium approaches.

Whether it will be a millennium of peace or war will depend to a large measure on the ability of the great religions, and Christianity in particular, to draw from within themselves all that makes for peace—the peace that, as Gordon Wilson knew so well, the God of Love wants for all his children.

The Anglican Communion

A lecture by Roger Symon, Canon Librarian of Canterbury Cathedral, to members of the congregation, November 20, 1997

In an informal moment during the 1988 Lambeth Conference the then Archbishop of Canterbury offered a prize to anyone in the Conference who could suggest a better name for the Communion than the Anglican Communion. As you can imagine, it took people by surprise, and perhaps it surprises you, too. Why should someone as Anglican as Archbishop Runcie suggest, even light-heartedly, that the name be changed? Perhaps because as Archbishop he has had eight years of direct exposure to the Anglican Communion, and to non-English forms of Anglicanism. Be that as it may, I want to share some of my exposure with you—having worked four years for the present Archbishop, and four years for his predecessor, as his Anglican Communion Secretary—and to reflect on some of the questions raised in my mind by my own direct exposure to many parts of the Anglican Communion.

You may be forgiven for thinking that Anglicanism is what goes on in the Church of England. The thought is quite natural. After all, there is no denying that in origin the word is connected to the word "English." But only a moment's thought will make you want to add that Anglicanism is that form of Church life that goes on in those Churches and Provinces that derive their existence, however remotely, from the Church of England. The point I want to make is that the Church of England does not own Anglicanism. Anglicans are proud of their tradition, but most Anglicans have never been to England, and we should not define Anglicanism in a way that excludes or undervalues the majority.

Being Anglican yourselves, then it will certainly occur to you from time to time to ask how appropriate it is to call your Church "Anglican," however much you can trace its historical development back to this country. For a Church to be named after a country is strange, especially to those who feel no other connection with the country concerned. For some the name is a quaint anomaly they can live with; for others, an occasional embarrassment; and for yet others, a downright liability that can create awkward political problems. For them this is no academic or theoretical question. If your diocese is situated in a country in which Britain and the West are regarded with suspicion, people wonder whether you do not in some way represent a foreign power. English Anglicans were sometimes an embarrassment to South African Anglicans in the dark days of apartheid because the Nationalist Government regarded the government of Mrs. Thatcher as its strongest ally, and with good reason.

Anglican Bishops in the Middle East know to their cost that public opinion makes no distinction between the Church in the West and governments in the West, especially when the Church is established by law and its Bishops appointed by the Prime Minister. I wonder how my friend the Anglican Bishop in Cairo is getting on these days. I guess he is having a tough time if the atrocities in Luxor and Cairo are part of a groundswell of resentment against the Christian West, because in the minds of the majority, Anglican Christianity belongs to the political West.

So the case for change is strong. And there is another argument. The balance of membership of the Communion is shifting, just as the center of faith itself has shifted—from the Middle East, where it started, to Europe, to the Americas, to Asia, and now in our own day to Africa. So Anglicanism is moving also, becoming less English in character, in numbers, and in self understanding. History assumes a smaller place in the decisions of its councils, and new ecumenical agreements are blurring the marks of ecclesiological identity. The Church of England is no longer normative of the faith and order of other Anglican Churches, and woe betide any Church of England representative at an international Anglican gathering who suggests or implies that the way things are done in England should set the standard for other Anglican Churches. Sadly this assumption of superiority has not entirely vanished. The present Bishop of Ely, Stephen Sykes, wrote about it:

> English Anglican condescension is simply intolerable. Much of it, of course, is quite unconscious, and if you are an Anglican and have no

idea to what I am referring, then you will have to seek help from your own non-Anglican friends. It is the effortless superiority of . . . those who occupy the high ground of English culture—or used to. Who own the cathedrals and ancient parish churches of this land, produced those literary masterpieces the Book of Common Prayer and the Authorized Version, claim for ourselves the rights of a pedigree of unbroken succession back to the Apostles, and crown the Sovereign of the land.

We also, of course, helped to destroy Ireland then forgot about it; persecuted and imprisoned Catholics and Nonconformists whilst congratulating ourselves on our comprehensive middle way; and in our own day when our Government invited vast numbers of Afro-Anglicans from the Caribbean, we failed to make them welcome and to foster their contribution to the Church's life.

(from *Unashamed Anglicanism: Authority & Ecclesiology.* Nashville: Dimensions for Living, 1995, p. 218)

Perhaps I could add on a personal note that before I came to Canterbury my own parish in West London would have been a shadow of itself without the members of West Indian origin who belonged to it.

I say these things not so much because one sometimes comes across an attitude of residual British colonialism, but because I believe that the Churches of the Communion have at least as much to give to the future of Anglicanism (whatever name we may give it) than does the Church of England from its own history, at least in terms of spiritual strength.

Now curiously there seems to be some connection between that spiritual strength and the social or economic conditions in which a Church is set. It is unwise to generalize, but where a Church is faced with political oppression or discrimination, Christian commitment sometimes seems to benefit; whereas, where the Church is in a "free" and economically advanced society, it attracts less support. For example, look at what happened in the Church in South Africa, or China, or Poland. In the Soviet Union it wasn't the Orthodox Church that withered away but Marxism itself. In South Africa the Churches played a decisive role in bringing about the new social order.

Extraordinary life

Again in an adverse economic climate the Church often seems to prosper. The experience of a Church or Province in Africa, in the "Developing World," or in "the two-thirds world" is so different from the experience of North American and North European Christians, and sometimes leads to extraordinary life and vigor. Inevitably, Churches' priorities are affected. It is not just that more Anglican Christians attend Church on Sunday in Nigeria, for example, than in any other Anglican Church. It has more to do with the contrasting circumstances in which Nigerian Anglicans minister. The context determines the Church's priorities and, in some cases, leads to a more vigorous sense of mission. So visitors from England are impressed by the vitality of Church life in Africa, and as institutional Church life declines in Europe, so momentum is passing to where numbers are rising, and the center of gravity of the Anglican Communion is shifting to other parts of the world.

But Englishness persists. One of my first visits to the Anglican Communion was in 1982, when I went to South Africa and visited most of the dioceses during a long tour. In Johannesburg the Bishop was holding a party at his house for people from the diocese, and he kindly invited me to join them. Looking around the room, I was surprised at the balance of white and black faces. There were many more whites that I had expected, and I remarked on this to one of the Archdeacons who was also present. He exclaimed, "But this is the English Church!" That remark has stuck in my mind ever since. He didn't even say the Anglican Church; he said the English Church. It was quite a shock! And it was said without qualification, comment, or regret, but as a fact he saw no reason to question.

So let us look at how the Anglican Communion emerged from its English roots, took its present shape, and indeed is still developing.

A global family

The global spread of Anglicanism approximately coincided with the expansion of English-speaking peoples into colonial territories. This happened in the Americas, it happened in Africa, it happened in Asia. Settlers, colonialists, and traders came from Britain, made their homes in distant colonies, and brought their religion with them. They would write to Bishops and friends back home and ask whether they could arrange for a clergyman to come out and minister to them. Indeed, the USPG was formed in 1701 with the express intention of finding and supplying Priests to minister to settlers. There was no interest in the early days in evangelizing those people who surrounded the small colonial communities. It was a Church for expatriates. And naturally any colony of people living overseas liked to keep alive its memory of home. So they set about recreating the English parish Church and all the trappings of Anglican tradition in strange surroundings. Now we see the consequences all over the world. Gothic and perpendicular styles of architecture began to appear, and inside of them one could hear the Book of Common Prayer, sing "Praise my soul the King of heaven," and listen to a choir in cassock and surplice singing Stainer, Stanford, and Wesley with a Bengali, Zulu, or Jamaican lilt. Religion was there to remind you of home, of the faraway rural village on the other side of the world.

So today there are all over the world—in the big cities, often in a prime central location, sometimes in a rather crumbling state, and looking mildly incongruous—English-style parish Churches amongst the suks, bazaars, and shacks of a large oriental city, or dwarfed by high-rise buildings of a modern city. Thus, Surrey was recreated in the Punjab, and Norman architecture transplanted to the center of Seoul.

The colonial state of affairs did not remain unchanged for long. Very soon the Brits began to take an interest in the natives. They launched into education in a big way, imitating traditions back home, and built big solid schools after the model of the English public school, and large hospitals and clinics, across the savannahs and deep into the bush. They clearly knew what they believed, and one sure belief was that they were here to stay. If you have visited the Indian subcontinent, you will know what I mean. In the days of the Raj, salaries were paid to clergy and Church officials as if they were civil servants. The imperial government had an ecclesiastical department that specialized in building huge Churches in the cantonments, or military quarters. I have not traveled widely in India and Pakistan, but I know what a burden it is for the modern Church to maintain these buildings without the official support they once

The Communion remains a curious mixture of Anglican tradition and local customs. An Anglican Mission Church in Mexico.

received—buildings like the Cathedral in Lahore, or cantonment Church in Peshawar. In the eyes of local people, the Anglican Church at its best meant good education, good medicine, and good Christian teaching. But mixed up with the wheat were some tares. It also meant an alien occupying power, colonization, the imposition of another culture, and the suppression of local ways.

Now I do not wish to sneer at those Church people who were part of this movement. Our Victorian ancestors in the Church had the very best of intentions and hopes, and none of us can do more than carry out with vigor and commitment what we believe we should do. What interests me is the way they saw their faith through their own particular cultural and historical lens. The interaction of culture and Gospel is a continuing, absorbing, and central issue for the Church today. Of course it is inevitable that our understanding of the Gospel should be filtered through our social environment. We cannot perceive Christ and the Gospel except through minds that have been shaped by historical influences over which we have had no control—whether doctrinal, political, or cultural.

A missionary church

Alongside the establishment of a pastoral and liturgical ministry to expatriate British colonizers, there came a more Evangelical and evangelistic missionary movement that we now associate with our missionary societies in Britain. The Church Mission Society (CMS), formed at the beginning of the eighteenth century like USPG, was essentially a lay movement. It grew from an awareness that English Christians had a responsibility for those amongst whom they lived overseas, a voluntary movement of mainly lay Anglicans.

British political imperialism does not account for the existence of every Province of the Communion. Some are the result of British commercial life. Britain has always had a strong commercial influence in South America. If you do not know Argentina, you may be surprised to learn that there are fourteen Anglican Churches in Buenos Aires, built for what used to be small colonies of British society. It may seem incongruous, but, as you may know, one suburb of Buenos Aires is called Hurlingham, which gives its name to the quintessentially English institution—the Club—where you can play cricket, lawn tennis, and polo, and eat strawberries and cream. English cultural traditions are often more keenly defended overseas than they are in England itself.

There are of course many Churches in the Communion that owe nothing to British imperial history. The Church in Korea, for example, although founded by an English Bishop, came as the result of an appeal to the Archbishop of Canterbury by the Anglican Bishops of China. It's another story of heroic Christian mission, and in 1993 the Church in Korea became an autonomous Province of the Communion. Also, Anglicanism spread as established Provinces sent missionaries to evangelise "new" territory—for example, from the American Episcopal Church in Central America to the Philippines and Liberia, and from the Australian and New Zealand Church to the South Pacific, Papua New Guinea, and Polynesia.

In all these ways Anglican missionaries have inevitably exported their faith in the clothes of the country from which they have come, reflecting their traditions and superficial customs as well as the faith and order of their home Church.

Inculturation

Let me give you an illustration. In October 1986 I attended the enthronement of Desmond Tutu as Archbishop of Cape Town. It was of course an unforgettable occasion and it took place in St. George's Cathedral, which in those days preserved the epitome of the English Cathedral musical tradition. They did it so superbly well that it is a shame to think of adapting it. They sang "I Was Glad" by Parry and other anthems that you will know well. But the new Archbishop had arranged for a choir of several hundred singers from Soweto to take part also. At the offertory this enormous choir launched into traditional African song, and at once the atmosphere was transformed. Replacing the formal, restrained, and dignified ways of traditional English worship, the whole congregation began to sway and dance as they sang. You felt the music had touched the African soul, and they were at last being themselves. Their own culture was put to the service of worship.

This missionary mixture of Christian gospel and English culture is of course well known and has been much mocked, but I want to assert two things: (1) the Gospel can never be culture-free, and (2) the devotion and commitment of many early missionaries was heroic-eccentric—saints and heroes who gave their lives in extraordinary circumstances, many of whom are revered in African Churches today.

Anglicans uphold the rights of disadvantaged groups, working to build a Church that transcends ethnic division and discrimination.

Although we should be proud of much missionary activity, there is also much of which we are now rightly critical and even ashamed. We have in the past shared deeply in the sin of racism, and some of the examples I could quote are too painful to mention. I can think of a churchwarden fifteen years ago in a "white" parish in Africa who said to me who there was a vacancy: "It matters more to us that the new Priest should be white than that he should be holy, godly, or good." When I was in Canada in 1994 with the Archbishop, we were told of the apology recently made by the Primate, Michael Peers, to the native peoples. We talked with native people, visited a Mohawk Chapel, and learned about their sufferings, and all that had been done to subjugate, if not destroy, their culture. All over the Communion the recognition of minorities is a feature of Anglican mission. In New Zealand they have even changed the Constitution of the Church in order to give the indigenous people a measure of autonomy. It is now called the Anglican Church of Aotearoa, New Zealand, and Polynesia.

Human dignity

Of course not all ethnic division in the Anglican Communion has come about from British colonial history. Ethnic prejudice and conflict remain one of the most terrifying and persistent evils in our world. Some of the problems of separate ethnic groups have come about from the normal patterns of emigration and demographic movement. I believe that in most places our Church is in the forefront of the struggle to overcome ethnic division. I think of dioceses like Sabah and Kuching in East Malaysia, or some of the dioceses in West Africa, or many parts of the Province of the Southern Cone of South America. In all these places you can find Anglican Churches upholding the rights of the minority or disadvantaged groups, and struggling to build a Church that transcends ethnic division and discrimination.

Wherever you look in the world, whether at India with its caste system, or Malaysia with its spectrum of ethnic groups, or indeed in North America or Europe, the same battle is being fought: the struggle to build a Church that is truly open to all—truly inclusive, truly local and catholic, and truly affirmative of local identities—but can still unite believers across them. The task is far from complete, and many of the questions still need better thought-out answers. How can the Church both respect local cultures and integrate them into one fellowship? How can the Church, which claims to be catholic, transcend nationality without one culture seeming to dominate the others? These are questions for Churches comprised not only of different ethnic groups, but also of different cultures.

Of course in many places it's not so much a case of two groups, one dominant and one inferior, but of a pluralism of many small groups. In New York the Bishop will tell you that in his diocese the Sunday liturgy is celebrated in a dozen different languages. Others can make similar claims. In these cases the Anglican Church is helping to affirm and encourage local cultures and strengthen local identity, by setting them within a universal Gospel.

It is worship that we chiefly think of when talk about culture and the Gospel. In the United Kingdom guitars and pop music have become symbols of an attempt to free the Church from the dominant Anglican culture. But there can be something superficial about that. There are deeper cultural issues. Sometimes at meetings Archbishop Tutu would ask me whether I had thrown away my watch yet, or (the implication was) whether I was still being driven by the Western demon of time. There are ethnic and national characteristics that we should rejoice in rather than try to annul. Many people have written about that African quality called "ubuntu," a quality of being human, a way of regarding others that is open and generous and warm. I was once told that in Swahili there is only one word for the two English words "stranger" and "guest." This is a fascinating insight into a very non-European culture.

So there are deeper things here, and the inculturation of faith and Church life has a long way to go, but Christians from other cultures help us to distinguish what in a culture is an acceptable variation, what is dubious, and what is contrary to the Gospel. In any worldwide Communion there are opportunities for cross-cultural fellowship, giving us the chance to see how different cultures highlight different aspects of the Gospel. In my view, too little work is being done to articulate these issues. What we need is more theological thinking, more deliberate attention to local custom in the light of the Gospel. I remember a conversation I once had in Accra with the Ghanaian theologian John Pobee, who talked to me about Christian theology and African thought forms and, in particular, the African tradition of reverence for ancestors and the doctrine of the communion of saints. It is in these areas of Christian thinking that the Church needs to address the interface of Gospel and culture and, where possible, to integrate the teachings of the Gospel and local tradition.

There is a danger that culture may assume too much importance. Culture can be pushed to the colorful margin of society. It can be thought of as what you lay on for tourists. Americans think English culture is city gents with bowler hats and furled umbrellas, or Beefeaters at the Tower of London, and the changing of the Guard at Buckingham Palace. African culture is Zulu tribal dancing, or Maasai women in traditional dress. But these things are folklore—quaint ceremonies, costumes, and customs that belong to the past. Do we not in fact all aspire to live in a technologically based culture, whether we live in Kigali or Kerala? Does not every Bishop in Uganda or Sri Lanka want to avail himself of reliable computer systems and good technology? And when the day comes that "development," as we are pleased to call it, comes to Africa, will it come at the expense of that wonderful variety and simplicity of life that we in the North admire so much, and that seems so close to Christian life?

Beyond 2000

So what is Anglicanism, or, more important, what is it going to become? We know were it has come from, we know where it can be found, but where is it going? The older Churches have much to learn from the younger. The intellectual complexity of Western theology has been tested by the primary concerns of Churches living in places where life is at a premium. If a Bishop is concerned day by day with how to feed his people (I think of Bishops ministering among the refugees in francophone Africa, or on the borders of Sudan and Uganda), that clarifies his theological priorities. If a Bishop is wrestling day in and day out with how to protect his people from political oppression (I am thinking of our Bishops in Jerusalem), that clarifies his understanding of Christian mission. If a Bishop is absorbed with his relations with Islamic leaders (I am thinking of Bishops in Pakistan and Malaysia), that clarifies his mind on the essence and uniqueness of the Gospel. I could go on because the majority of Anglican dioceses witness in such circumstances.

But it is from such Bishops and such Churches of the Communion that we stand to learn a lot about the future of Anglicanism. I believe theology will be an effete and weak affair without their participation, and we need to hear what they are saying. South Africa has already taught us that the struggle for justice is a necessary part of Christian spirituality. The sincerity of our faith is rightly challenged by fellow Anglicans in the Developing World if we are not in some way serving the poor and advocating their cause in our own society. Anglicanism cannot be defined without reference to such contemporary Christian experience. Our Communion is largely a suffering Communion, where prayer and theology are hammered out in the context of deprivation and injustice.

One final word: We are a fellowship of autonomous, self-governing Provinces, or groups of dioceses. Out of the vigor of Anglican missionary activity in the nineteenth century, new dioceses were created, at first with an English Bishop and English missionaries. Then, as more local Priests were trained, local Bishops were elected. Now very few expatriate Bishops can be found. At first a diocese covered huge distances, but gradually, as time went by, a large diocese would subdivide into several smaller dioceses, and new Bishops would be consecrated. As that happened a group of local dioceses would seek the permission of their former Archbishop to form their own self-governing, autonomous Province with their own Archbishop. Thus, in the 1950s Archbishop Fisher was busy granting independence to new Anglican Provinces in East Africa, West Africa, and Central Africa—all of them now divided again into smaller Provinces. More recently new Provinces have been created in Korea, with its three Dioceses, and in Southeast Asia (Singapore, West Malaysia, Sabah, and Kuching) and the Philippines. The Anglican Communion also enjoys the closest relations with those Churches of South India, North India, Pakistan, and Bangledesh, of which Anglicans were founding members with Churches of other denominations. These Churches point the way that we pray all Anglicans will one day follow, until we find the unity in Christ we have been promised.

Untidy but lovable

The Communion remains a curious untidy mixture of Anglican tradition (with English characteristics) and local customs. There is no central jurisdiction, only an obligation to consult one another. The Lambeth Conference meeting in Canterbury next July will once again address many traditional Anglican concerns. What are the doctrinal obligations of membership? What is the irreducible core of doctrine without which no Church can claim to be Anglican? And who decides who is in and who is out? Ought there to be an Anglican Communion Synod, just as there is a local, diocesan, and national synod, with authority to take decisions on behalf of us all? These are some of the questions Lambeth will face, under the leadership of the Archbishop of Canterbury. His office of honorary leadership is necessarily concerned with the unity, integrity, and coherence of the Communion, and this Lambeth Conference will return to these questions as all previous Conferences have done. The Communion has agreed statements, a strong tradition, and historical bonds, and it will certainly wish to retain the form of universal primacy associated with the office of the Archbishop.

I believe it is urgently important for our Church to strengthen its unity within the Communion, and to pursue a wider unity with other Communions. In this way we can signal to the world that the Gospel is truly universal, and demonstrate to people from all corners of the globe that the Lord is calling us into a single new humanity in him.

Anglican Temperament

John H. Westerhoff

Temperament refers to a tradition's characteristic ways of thinking and behaving. Anglican temperament is comprehensive, ambiguous, open-minded, intuitive, aesthetic, moderate, naturalistic, historical, and political.

Comprehensive

Anglicans affirm a principle of comprehensiveness or the *via media* (literally, "nothing too much," or "the middle way"), that is, the conviction that truth is known and guarded by maintaining the tension between counter-opposite statements concerning truth. This principle is exemplified in the conviction that Jesus was fully human and at the same time fully divine, in the Anglican commitment to being simultaneously both fully Catholic and Protestant, and in the stated necessity of holding in tension personal freedom and communal responsibility. While applying this principle of comprehensiveness is extremely difficult to do in practice, the struggle to do so is an important aspect of our tradition.

Anglicans, therefore, affirm both the sacred and the secular; material and nonmaterial reality; the speculative illumination of the mind and the affective illumination of the heart; the possibility of a direct, unmediated experience of God and the indirect mediated experience of God; the transcendent mystery of God and the immanent intimacy of God; and the contradictory convictions that faith is a gift that results from participation in the sacraments and faith is a necessary precondition for participation in the sacraments.

Furthermore, this principle provides a means to resolve what may appear to be severe disagreements. For example, Anglicans contend that we live into our baptism by the process of becoming who we already are. This conviction makes possible the affirmation of two conflicting convictions, namely, that every transformational benefit is given to us fully at our baptism and that we must engage throughout our lifetime in efforts to achieve the benefits of baptism.

Ambiguous

The category of ambiguity has often been misunderstood. It is not a political category that can be used to justify incompetence and sloppiness. It is rather a theological category that makes possible living with what may appear to be irreconcilable differences. To

The highest desires of true civilisation are to be found in religious hope and expression.

affirm the ambiguous implies that when we are faced with new experiences or complex issues we will remain open to various interpretations and demonstrate a willingness to live with uncertainty of meaning until a resolution can be found.

Indeed, Anglicans affirm an openness to all experience and believe in the developed capacity to be sensitive and accept what our senses tell us even when they do not fit into neat comprehensible established categories, that is, are ambiguous, incomprehensible, obscure, or strange. Anglicans are able to tolerate theological and ethical messiness; we do not need to have everything resolved or settled immediately. With a developed sensibility we tend to be more inductive and pragmatic than deductive and systematic. We are willing to live with trial and error as a means toward establishing truth. Anglicans believe that conflict, when handled in reconciling ways, is healthy and not to be avoided. Indeed, conflict is a necessary aspect of the theological-ethical task.

This ability to live with ambiguity helps us to deal with situations in which two or more biblical texts, theological principles, or ethical norms appear logically incompatible. When this does occur, we are able to wait patiently (neither fleeing the situation nor fighting it), to pray with a discerning heart, and to listen with an open mind until the conflict can be reconciled through the aid of the Holy Spirit.

Open-minded

Anglicans encourage a searching, questioning, reasonable mind that is always open to new insights and change. We listen carefully to everyone, search for wisdom everywhere, take seriously the secular world and its work, and recognize that contemporary knowledge is not necessarily in conflict with faith and indeed may offer wisdom. Of course, it needs to be noted that each of these character traits of Anglicans has its negative side that can manifest itself in serious distortions. For example, being open-minded can result in the uncritical acceptance of all truth claims, and the blessing of the secular world and its understandings and ways. Similarly, the theological ethical category of ambiguity can be used to avoid all decisions on what is good and true. Furthermore, we need to be careful to include all these character traits and not be selective.

Intuitive

While never being antiintellectual, Anglicans are more at home in the intuitive way of thinking and knowing than is the intellectual. We prefer art to philosophy and are more at home in the world of symbol, myth, and ritual than in systematic theology; more at home with liturgy that makes use of the arts (drama, dance, music, poetry, and the visual arts) than with discursive prose; and more at home with the feminine than the masculine dimensions of life. Anglicans affirm the anagogical, the metaphorical, the paradoxical, the symbolic, and the prerational in dealing with human experience. Recognizing that human nature and society are more deeply motivated by images and tabulations than ideas and concepts, we are apt to emphasize the imagination while keeping in tension objective consciousness and rational ideas with subjective consciousness and nonrational impressions.

Aesthetic

Truth, goodness, and beauty are related to each other in that the presence of one is judged by the presence of the other two. For example, beauty can be defined as a revelation of the presence (priestly) or the absence (prophetic) of goodness and truth. While some traditions emphasize truth and goodness, Anglicans have made beauty the doorway into truth and goodness. We have a strong respect for and belief in beauty and holiness and righteousness. Money spent on beauty, priestly and prophetic, is justified in so far as it is our way of revealing and advocating truth and goodness. Our Churches are intended to be works of art, and we make every effort to ensure that the arts used in our Churches are of high quality. Artists have always been at home in our congregations and played a significant role in our worship and common life.

Moderate

Anglicans believe that they are called to live a godly (to manifest the divine image in ourselves), righteous (to live in a right relationship to God and neighbor), and sober life. That means that Anglicans typically avoid extravagance, extremes, and excessiveness in any aspect of personal and Communion life, thought or emotion. We are a people of moderation and restraint who model a temperate, balanced, reasonable approach to life. It is a life in which prayer, work, study, and play have a rhythm.

Naturalistic

Anglicans have a reverence for and take a delight in the natural earthy rhythms of life, the seasons and their changes, the natural world and all of creation. Not only have we historically affirmed natural theology and natural law, means by which God has made some knowledge of his will and his ways possible to all reasonable human beings, but we have always taken seriously the contributions of the natural sciences to human life. Through the years our poets have filled us with an awareness of nature and ecology. We have always taken pride in using live flowers and real candles, and in surrounding ourselves with natural things in the Church. At our best we have been committed to the ecological movement.

Historical

Anglicans have a great sense of history and a desire to honor tradition. At times this tempts us to turn our Churches into museums and refuse to remodel them for more faithful contemporary worship, but mostly it has encouraged us to take the past seriously and respect what we can learn from a careful reflection on the past, as well as strive to maintain our roots in Anglican history and culture. This historic consciousness is manifested in our concern for apostolic succession as the way to link the Church with its past.

Political

And lastly, our English history has made us a political Church. That is, we value the civic virtues and affirm free, peaceful, public debate as a basis for political unity. We believe that such civic debate should encourage and that the Church is an appropriate place to engage in it. We believe that the Church has an obligation to attempt to influence social, political, and economic life. We, therefore, have always shown a concern for the government and its policies and actions, assumed responsibility for participation in public life, and accepted leadership roles in politics. Furthermore, we have emphasized that our ministry, the context in which we serve God and represent Christ and his Church, is our daily life and work.

Canterbury Cathedral in History
Canon D. Ingram III

St. Augustine, the first Archbishop of Canterbury, is said by the historian Bede to have found the ruins of a Romano-British Church on the site of the present Cathedral, and to have rebuilt this and set up his archiepiscopal chair here. The Saxon Cathedral that developed from this modern beginning was destroyed by fire in 1067 and almost at once was replaced by a grandiose Romanesque Benedictine Church constructed during the primacy of the great Norman monk-Archbishops Lanfranc and Anselm. This splendid Church, consecrated in 1130, was the scene of the murder of St. Thomas Becket in 1170, and only four years later a great fire consumed the

Pilgrims visit holy places to renew themselves through contemplation and meditation. In Canterbury.

eastern arc of the Church, the monastic quire (sparing the great crypt and the eastern towers, which still remain, and the Norman nave, which was to last for two hundred years more). In place of the gutted quire there arose in the next decade or so the magnificent building in the French Gothic style that set a fashion for all of England. It was the creation of two great architects: the Frenchman William of Sens, and William "the Englishman." The body of St. Thomas was transported in 1220 to the Trinity Chapel, built over the eastern crypt, and lay there in a splendid golden shrine as the object of devotion to multitudes of pilgrims for the next three hundred years. To the later Middle Ages belongs the superb perpendicular Gothic nave, the Cloisters, and above all, the great central tower known as Bell Harry. Less than forty years after the completion of this tower, the Middle Ages came to a decisive end with the destruction of the famous shrine of St. Thomas and the ending of the pilgramages in 1538. This was followed in 1540 by the dissolution of the great Benedictine monastery, which had dominated the life of the city for so long.

Some months later a new foundation was inaugurated with the establishment of a chapter of deans and canons, supported by other officers, lay and clerical (many of them ex-monks). There began a century of profound religious controversy in which every part of the British Isles and most of Europe were involved.

This came to a climax with the sacking of the Cathedral by the Puritans in 1642, the dissolution of the Cathedral chapter, and the execution of King Charles I in 1649. It was not until 1660 that the monarchy was restored and with it the Church of England. Life returned to the Cathedral, the fabric was repaired, and daily services were resumed with the reestablishment of the chapter and staff.

For the next two hundred years a kind of spiritual lassitude fell upon the Church in general and the Cathedral in particular. It was not until midway through the nineteenth century, with a series of energetic Archbishops at the head of Church affairs and equally vigorous deans in the Cathedral, that new life began to transform the life and work of the Cathedral Church of Christ in Canterbury. Restoration of the fabric, revival of pilgrimage (now on ecumenical lines), a reordering of its liturgical services, and a great renaissance of its music have been conspicuous marks of this new period of life and vitality.

George Herbert's Hymns
Poet, hymn-writer, priest

Antiphon

Let all the world in every corner sing,
MY GOD AND MY KING.
The heavens are not too high,
His raise may thither fly:
The earth is not too low,
His praises there may grow.

Let all the world in every corner sing,
MY GOD AND MY KING.
Let all the world in every corner sing,
MY GOD AND MY KING.
The church with psalms must shout,
No door can keep them out;
But above all, the heart
Must bear the longest part.
Let all the world in every corner sing,
MY GOD AND MY KING.

Antiphon

Praised be the God of Love,
Here below, and here above:
Who has dealt his mercies so,
To his friend, and to his foe;

That both grace and glory tend
Us of old, and us in the end.
The great shepherd of the fold
Us did make, for us was sold.

He our foes in pieces break;
Him we touch; and him we take.
Wherefore since that he is such,
We adore and we do crouch.

Lord, thy praises shall be more.
We have none, and we no store.
Praise be the God alone
Who hath made two folds of one.

The Elixir

Teach me, my God and King,
In all things thee to see,
And what I do in anything,
To do it as for Thee.

[Not rudely, as a beast,
To run into an action;
But still to make thee prepossest,
And give it his perfection.]

A man that looks on glass,
On it may stay his eye;
Or if it pleaseth, though it pass
And then the heaven espy.

All may of Thee partake;
Nothing can be so mean,
Which with this tincture, FOR THY SAKE,
Will not grow bright and clean.

A servant with this clause
Makes drudgery divine;
Who sweeps room, as for thy laws,
Makes that and th'action fine.

This is the famous stone
That turneth all to gold,
Far that which God doth touch and own
Cannot for less be told.

*(The verses in square brackets
are usually omitted from hymnbooks.)*

Praise

King of glory, King of peace. I will love thee;
And that love may never cease,
I will move thee.

Thou hast granted my request,
Thou hast heard me;
Thou didst note my working breast,
Thou hast spared me.

Wherefore with my utmost art
I will sing Thee;
And the cream of all my heart
I will bring Thee.

Though my sins against me cried,
Thou didst clear me;
And alone, when they replied,
Thou didst hear me.

Seven whole days, not one in seven
I will praise Thee:
In my heart, though not in heaven,
I can raise Thee.

[Thou grew'st soft and moist with tears,
Thou relentedst;
And when justice called for fears,
Thou dissentedst.]

Small it is in this poor sort
To enroll Thee;
Even eternity is too short
To extol Thee.

The Call

Come, my Way, my Truth, my Life;
Such a Way as gives us breath,
Such a Truth as ends all strife,
Such a Life as killeth death.

Come, my Light, my Feast, my Strength;
Such a Light as shows a feast,
Such a Feast as mends in length,
Such a Strength as makes his guest.

Come, my Joy, my Love, my Heart;
Such a Joy as none can move,
Such a Love as none can part,
Such a Heart as joys in love.

The 23rd Psalm

The God of love my shepherd is,
And he that doth me feed;
While He is mine and I am His,
What can I want or need?

He leads me to the tender grass,
Where I both feed and rest;
Then to the streams that gently pass;
In both I have the best.

Or if I stray, he doth convert
And bring my mind in frame;
And all this not for my desert,
But for His holy name.

Yea, in death's shady black abode,
Well may I walk, not fear;
For thou art with me, and Thy rod
To guide, Thy staff to bear.

[Nay, Thou dost make me sit and dine
E'en in my enemies' sight;
My head with oil, my cup with wine,
Runs over day and night.]

Surely the sweet and wondrous lobe
Shall measure all my days;
And as it never shall remove.
So neither shall my praise.

Glossary of Terms

Acolyte An altar assistant; server at the liturgy.

Alleluia Hebrew for "Praise the Lord."

Altar The table placed centrally in front of the congregation where the Priest celebrates Holy Communion. (Some use the term "Holy Table.")

Anglican A member of a Church belonging to the Anglican Communion (adjective commonly used as a noun), also called Episcopalian.

Anglican Communion Group of Churches worldwide with historic and present links with the Archbishop of Canterbury.

Anglican Consultative Council International body of representatives from the Churches of the Anglican Communion that meets approximately every two to three years. Address: Partnership House, 157 Waterloo Road, London SE1 8UT (Tel: 0171-620 1110).

Anointing of the Sick A rite or sacrament administered during worship or as needed in emergencies. Oil is used having been blessed during Holy Week.

Antiphon A short refrain, usually from Scripture, used with the Psalms.

Apocrypha Often called the "hidden books" of the Old Testament. Used in most Anglican lectionaries.

Archbishop Leading Bishop with authority over a Province. In some Provinces called Presiding Bishop, Primus, or Prime Bishop.

Archdeacon A senior member of the clergy responsible to the Diocesan Bishop for an Archdeaconry. The Archdeacon usually instructs new incumbents, shares the pastoral care of the clergy and does much practical, legal, and administrative work.

Ashes Symbol of penance and reconciliation. Used especially on the first day of Lent.

Augustine First Archbishop of Canterbury—A.D. 597

Aumbry Also "Ambry." A small recess in the wall of a Church or sacristy in which the consecrated bread and wine or holy oils might be kept.

Banns of Marriage Procedure whereby the names of those from a particular parish who are proposing to marry are given out publicly in the parish Church on three Sundays shortly before the wedding is due. Legal objections to the marriage can then be lodged.

Baptism Often called "christening": a ceremony by which an individual infant or adult is received into membership of the Church. Water is usually poured over the head of the person being baptised, though sometimes candidates are immersed in water.

Bible The Inspired word of God, the Old and New Testaments, the Scriptures.

Bishop Chief minister (of a diocese) with spiritual oversight of clergy and laypeople. Bishops are first and most senior of the three Holy Orders of the ordained ministry in the Church. A diocesan Bishop often has the help of other Bishops.

Book of Common Prayer Thomas Cranmer's 1662 masterpiece containing liturgy, prayers, psalms, ceremonies, and the Ordinal. Various Provinces have official revisions now in use.

Bowing Showing respect or devotion to the altar or cross; in Catholic usage "genuflection," bending the knee, is customary to honour the Blessed Sacrament.

Calendar The holy days and saints days commemorated by the Churches.

Candle Used in Churches and worship symbolising the presence and light of Christ. Often lit as a symbol of prayer and intercession.

Canon (a) Law of the Church; (b) Residentiary Canon, Honorary Canon, Minor Canon, and Lay Canon of a Cathedral.

Canterbury Cathedral Mother Church of the Anglican Communion, seat of the Archbishop of Canterbury.

Canticle A song, usually from Scripture, (e.g., Magnificat, Benedictus).

Cassock Long garment, usually black, worn by clergy.

Cathedral Principal Church building of a diocese, staffed by a dean (or provost) and chapter, where the diocesan Bishop has his Cathedral ("seat" or "throne").

Catholic Church members who stress the sacraments, personal devotion, the communion of saints, the apostolic tradition and various degrees of ceremony in worship.

Chalice Cup used in Holy Communion.

Chancel In most Churches that part of the building in front of the nave that encloses the sanctuary where the altar is placed. The choir often sits in the chancel.

Chapel (a) A subsidiary "Church within a Church" in a Church building, often where weekday services are held; (b) A place of worship within an institution (e.g., school, hospital, prison).

Chaplain (a) Priest, Deacon, or layperson in a special community such as a school, college, university, prison, hospital, the armed forces, industry, and so forth; (b) Priest, Deacon, or layperson who assists a Bishop in administration or on ceremonial occasions.

Chapter (a) Corporate title for the dean and canons of a Cathedral; (b) corporate title for the clergy of a deanery.

Charismatic Refers to individuals or groups within the Church who stress a direct experience of the Holy Spirit of God within their lives and worship. Referred to collectively as the Charismatic, "Pentecostal," or "Renewal" movements in Churches.

Chasuble The outermost garment worn by Bishops and Priests in celebrating the Eucharist.

Chism Oil blessed by a Bishop in Holy Week, used for sacramental rites.

Christian Stewardship Scheme to encourage Church members to respond to God's love and generosity by giving their time, talents, and money on a regular basis for the needs of the Church and society.

Church (a) Corporate body of Christians linked by a common tradition and institutional structure; (b) Corporate name for all

Christians throughout the world (thus the worldwide Church); (c) Place where Christians meet for worship (thus a Church building).

Church Army Organisation of trained laypeople within the Church who assist in parishes or engage in various mission and social projects throughout the country. Men are "Captains"; women are "Sisters." Headquarters Address: Independents Road, Blackheath, London SE8 9LG (Tel: 0181-318 1226).

Clergy General name for all ordained ministers.

Columba Patron Saint of the Celtic Christian tradition, associated with Iona.

Communion A group of Churches worldwide who regard themselves as one Christian family (e.g., the Anglican Communion).

Confirmation Sacramental rite at which a Bishop presides, in which baptized members of the Church affirm their faith and are endowed with grace through the laying on of hands.

Consecration (a) A ceremony by which a group of Bishops ordain a Priest to be Bishop; (b) Central action in the service of Holy Communion when bread and wine are set apart for sacred use before being shared among members of a congregation; (c) Ceremony conducted by a Bishop by which a new Church building or cemetery is exclusively set apart for sacred use. Many modern Churches are dedicated rather than consecrated, especially when they are designed for community as well as Church use.

Convent House occupied by a community of nuns.

Cope An often elaborate cape worn in procession.

Crosier The crook-shaped staff of Bishops, sometimes carried also by abbots and abbesses.

Curate Deacon or Priest appointed to assist the incumbent or take charge of a parish temporarily during a vacancy or while the incumbent is incapacitated.

Cursillo A popular renewal movement in many Anglican Churches. A Cursillo event lasts three days.

Deacon A special order of ministry for men and women associated with Christian service.

Dean (a) Senior Priest in charge of a Cathedral; (b) Title given to senior clergy of some colleges in universities or in geographic areas in a diocese.

Deanery (a) A collection of parishes over which the rural dean has oversight; (b) House occupied by the dean of a Cathedral.

Dedication (a) Ceremony by which a new building or other major asset (e.g., bells, Church organ, new Church furnishing) is blessed for Church use; (b) The saint or event after which a Church is named.

Deposition Removal of an ordained minister from the exercise of Holy Orders when found guilty of a disciplinary offence. A minister so deposed may in no circumstances carry out any priestly functions.

Deprivation Removal of an ordained minister from any ecclesiastical office held when found guilty of a disciplinary offence.

Diocesan Bishop The Bishop in charge of a diocese.

Diocese Main administrative and pastoral area in the Church.

Ecclesial Pertaining to the Church as a theological concept; from the Greek/Latin *ecclesia.*

Ecclesiastical Pertaining to the Church in its institutional sense.

Ecumenical Movement General name given to the efforts by the various denominations to grow together and reestablish one Christian Church throughout the world.

Enthronement Ceremony by which a diocesan Bishop is received and welcomed in the Cathedral. Nowadays sometimes called installation or investiture.

Episcopacy The system of Church government involving Bishops.

Episcopalian See Anglican.

Episcopate (a) The Bishops collectively; (b) The office of Bishops or the time in office of a particular Bishop.

Established Church Because the Church of England is the "state" Church, some of its legislation has to be approved by Parliament. Bishops, Deans, and some residentiary canons are appointed by the Sovereign on the advice of the Prime Minister. Incumbents have a pastoral responsibility towards all residents in their parishes and not just to Church members. The twenty-six most senior diocesan Bishops also have seats in the House of Lords. However, the Church of England receives no financial assistance from the state apart from some state aid towards the maintenance and repair of outstanding parish Churches and Cathedrals.

Eucharist From the Greek word meaning "thanksgiving," a title for Holy Communion or Mass.

Evangelical Often used to refer to those Church members who stress the primacy of the Bible, the importance of personal conversion, and the doctrine of justification by faith.

Evangelisation The proclamation of the Gospel of Christ especially to those who have never heard it.

Evangelism The special responsibility of the Church locally and nationally to explain the Christian message of good news about Jesus Christ to those who have not heard it.

Evangelist A trained and authorized person who may be admitted to the office of Evangelist and have special responsibility for evangelism.

Evensong A form of Anglican worship consisting of psalms, Bible readings, and prayers, said daily in the evening by the clergy but frequently extended with hymns and a sermon to form the main evening service in a parish Church on Sundays. Otherwise known as "Evening Prayer."

Fasting A form of penance, sacrifice, and purifying. Called for in many prayer books for Ash Wednesday and Good Friday.

Font Item of furniture in a Church building, essentially in the form of a basin, where the sacrament of baptism is administered.

Holy Communion The distinctively Christian service of worship during which bread and wine consecrated by a Bishop or Priest are shared among members of the congregation who are confirmed, or admitted to communion, or who are communicant members of other denominations. Also called the Eucharist, the Lord's Supper, or the Mass.

Holy Orders The orders of ordained ministry: Bishops, Priests, Deacons.

Homily A short sermon or address.

House Groups Prayer, study, and fellowship gatherings within a congregation.

Incense Used in many religious rites, the smoke being considered symbolic of prayer and purification.

Inhibition Suspension of clergy from exercising the functions of their order for a specific time when they have been found guilty of a disciplinary offence.

Intercession Form of prayer during a service of worship expressing Christian concern for the needs of the world.

Laity General term for Church members (other than clergy).

Lambeth Conference Meeting of Bishops of the Anglican Communion held roughly every ten years since 1867. (Lambeth Palace is the official residence of the Archbishop of Canterbury.)

Lay Adjective derived from the Greek *laos*, meaning "of the people of God," commonly used of Church members who are not ordained.

Laying on of Hands The imposition of hands by a person ministering to another for prayers or healing.

Lectern Bookstand in a Church from which the Bible is read during worship. Sometimes called an "ambo."

Litany Sequence of prayers and intercessions during a service of worship in the form of a dialogue between the minister and the congregation, often in procession.

Mass An alternative name for Holy Communion, used in the Catholic tradition in the Church.

Mattins A form of Anglican worship consisting of psalms, Bible readings, and prayers, said daily in the morning, but also sometimes extended with hymns and a sermon. Otherwise known as "Morning Prayer." Alternative spelling "Matins."

Metropolitan Title of a Bishop who has special oversight over a group of dioceses or Province.

Mission The task of the Church and individual Christians to show other people the love of God by word and deed.

Mitre The liturgical headdress and part of the insignia of a Bishop.

Monastery House occupied by a community of monks.

Monk Male member of a religious order.

Nave The main body of a Church building where the congregation sits.

Nun Female member of a religious order.

Ordination Ceremony by which Priests and Deacons are commissioned. A Bishop always presides. A Bishop is also ordained and consecrated.

Parochial Church Council Elected governing body of a parish, usually chaired by the incumbent. Called "Vesty" in some places.

Paten The dish, now usually of silver, gold, or pottery, on which the bread is placed at the celebration of the Eucharist.

Pectoral Cross Cross worn by a Bishop.

Pilgrimage Visiting a holy place for prayer or retreat. An act of personal or communal devotion associated with a saint or historic event.

Priest Second order of ordained ministry.

Primate Title given to the Archbishop, or equivalent, of a Province.

Province Area of the Church under the authority of an Archbishop or equivalent—consisting of a number of dioceses.

Pulpit Elevated position within a Church building from which the sermon is preached.

Reader Layperson trained and licensed to preach and take services and assist in pastoral work in a parish. Normally this work is done without pay.

Rector A title for a parish Priest.

Religious Orders Men or women, clergy or laity, who bind themselves in a lifelong commitment and fellowship according to a monastic discipline or rule. Many groups (known as communities) follow the traditional rules (e.g., Benedictines [monks and nuns] and Franciscans [friars and sisters]). Members of religious orders are commonly addressed as "Brother" or "Sister," though "Father" continues to be used for Priests.

Retreat A time of prayer and contemplation; leaving normal activities for quiet and solitude.

Sacrament One of the ceremonies of the Church through which Christians believe God acts in a particularly significant way (e.g., baptism, Holy Communion, Penance, Confirmation, Holy Orders, Unction, and Marriage).

Sacristy A room in a Church, often used as a vestry, where the vessels used in Holy Communion are normally kept.

Sanctuary Name sometimes given to the area in a Church building where the altar or holy table stands.

Seminary A place of training for the ministry—called a theological college.

Sermon Lecture or address delivered during a service of worship by a Bishop, Priest, Deacon, reader, or other licensed preacher, designed to inform or inspire the congregation on matters of Christian faith or concern.

Server Layperson in attendance on a Bishop or Priest during public worship, especially at the Holy Communion. Called "acolytes."

Stole A liturgical vestment consisting of a long, narrow strip of cloth.

Surplice A liturgical vestment of white linen, with wide sleeves.

Thurible A metal vessel for the ceremonial burning of incense.

Tithing The biblical mandate for giving ten percent of one's income to support Church work or charity.

Verger In practice the caretaker of a Church building, full-time, part-time, or honorary. A verger often has a role in escorting the clergy as they move about the Church during a service of worship.

Vicar Title given to parish Priests of certain parishes.

Vigil Meaning "watching"—a time of prayer on the eve of a holy day, or a designated "watch" or prayer, as on Maundy Thursday.

Visitation Formal visit by a diocesan Bishop, Archdeacon, or rural dean to a parish or group of parishes at which the incumbent and/or churchwardens have to give an account of the affairs of their parish. Most frequently refers to the annual Archdeacon's visitation at which the churchwardens of a parish are admitted to office, and the clergy and the churchwardens hear the Archdeacon's charge.

Walsingham England's Nazareth, an Anglican centre of retreat and prayer in England honouring the Incarnation with special honour to Mary, Mother of Jesus.

Water Used in baptism for sprinkling, pouring, or immersion; also known as "holy water," used as a reminder of baptism.

Way of the Cross A devotion based on the Passion, death, and resurrection of Jesus. Also called "Stations," marking fourteen "stages" in the Passion.

World Council of Churches International organisation, founded in 1948, linking most major Christian Churches worldwide with the Roman Catholic Church as observers.

CANTERBURY CITY CENTRE

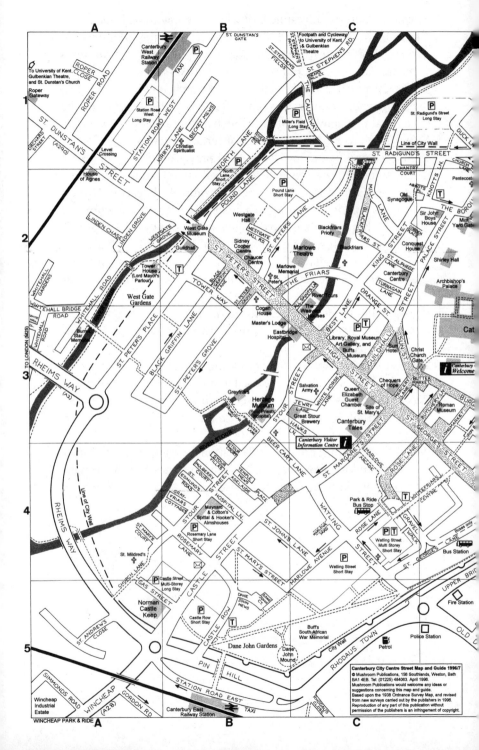

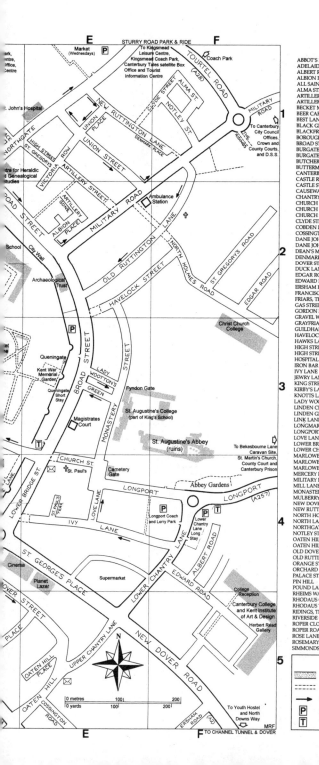

STREET INDEX

This map and information was put together from local surveys carried out by the publishers in 1996. All information was checked at the time of going to press. Every reasonable care has been taken to ensure that the information given is correct, and we hope that this publication will help to make your visit a pleasant and carefree one. Please address any comments or suggestions to the publishers.

KEY

Pedestrian Area	*i* Information Centre
Footpath	Post Office
One Way Street	Church
P Car Park	Petrol Station
T Toilet	Disabled Facilities

The Old Palace remains as a stately reminder of the Anglican Communion's history.

Through the sacrament of baptism, we are made members of Christ's body, the Church, and inheritors of the kingdom of God. From mural at the Cathedral of the Holy Trinity, Port-au-Prince, Haiti.

Affirm Anew the Threefold Name

Kingsfold   D.C.M.

English Traditional Melody

The Lambeth Conference Hymn

Affirm Anew the Threefold Name

(Suggested tune: Kingsfold)

Affirm anew the threefold Name
of Father, Spirit, Son,
our God whose saving acts proclaim
a world's salvation won.
In him alone we live and move
and breath and being find,
the wayward children of his love
who cares for humankind.

Declare in all the earth his grace,
to every heart his call,
the living Lord of time and place
whose love embraces all.
So shall his endless praise be sung,
his teaching truly heard,
and every culture, every tongue,
receive his timeless word.

Confirm our faith in this our day
amid earth's shifting sand,
with Christ as Life and Truth and Way,
a Rock on which to stand;
the one eternal Son and Lord
by God the Father given
the true and lie-imparting Word,
the Way that leads to heaven.

Renew once more the ancient fire,
let love our hearts inflame;
renew, restore, unite, inspire
the church that bears your name;
one Name exalted over all,
one Father, Spirit, Son,
O grant us grace to heed your call
and in that Name be one.

© *Timothy Dudley-Smith*

The Anglican Communion Secretariat
Partnership House
157 Waterloo Road
London SEI 8UT England

Telephone (0171) 620-1110
Fax (0171) 620-1070
Web address: www.anglicancommunion.org